MW01037916

The Dreamer and the Fantasy Relationship

NATALIE LUE

Published by Naughty Girl Media

Natalie Lue asserts the moral right to be identified as the author of this work.

Copyright 2013 Natalie Lue

Cover design by Lulabird Creative.

All rights reserved, including the right of reproduction in whole or in part in any form. No part of this publication may be reproduced, stored in a retrieval system, or transmitted, in any form or by any means, electronic, mechanical, photocopying, recording, or otherwise, without the prior written permission of the author.

ISBN: 1492832529
ISBN-13: 9781492832522

For NicNac

CONTENTS

A QUICK HONEST CONVERSATION

WITH YOURSELF

Do you get attached very quickly? In fact, do you get attached to someone or the idea of having a relationship with them before you've even been on a date?

Do you ruminate and struggle to 'get over someone' even if you only went on a few (or even no) dates?

Is your idea of 'getting out there' and meeting someone searching the internet?

If what you envisioned would happen or were told would happen, didn't happen do you struggle to get over it? Do you agonise and stew over what you see as a rejection of you and the future that you've been robbed of?

Have you been in a relationship where the bulk of, or even all, communication was by text, email, instant messenger, Facebook messaging, or even direct messages via Twitter?

Have you had someone tell you that you've imagined your involvement with them to be more than it actually is?

Have you tracked your ex (or even all your exes) online?

1

Have you had an involvement span years (or months) where you saw the other person infrequently, even if you lived in the same area code, state, or within an hour or two's travelling distance?

Do you have a compulsion to reply to texts and emails despite the person's minuscule overall efforts and the lack of meaningful content within the messages?

Do you see or hear something that *should* change your perception of a person and your expectations for the type of relationship you thought you'd have... then ignore the information?

Do you spend more time thinking about the type of relationship you should have, or contemplating the types of things your partner *must* do to fulfil you than you do actually living a relationship or making choices that reflect your vision and expectations?

If you answered 'yes' to even one of these questions, it's time to go on a fantasy diet. If you answered 'maybe', you may be having difficulty admitting the full truth, or don't recognise your own behaviour. If you answered 'no', but what you really mean is 'yes', it's time for you to come back to earth.

INTRODUCTION

When you've found yourself struggling to get over a relationship that didn't get off the ground, was unreciprocated, or largely virtual, you may not realise that you've been involved in a fantasy relationship, although you may have uttered something along the lines of, *'I can't figure out what was real and what was fake!'* While some people do the atypical fantasy and conjure up a relationship and a connection that doesn't and never did exist, many mix fantasy with sprinklings of reality – this is what I'm exploring in *The Dreamer and the Fantasy Relationship*.

Since September 2005, I've been writing baggagereclaim.com, a site where I help people make sense of unhealthy relationships and adopt more beneficial habits and perspectives, for better experiences and improved self-esteem. Over this time, I've come across an increasing number of people who are stuck in a sustained period of continuing a 'connection' mentally, after it's ceased in real life, with the help of the internet, texts, email, Facebook, Twitter, dating sites et al, plus those who use the flimsiest of connections as a springboard to create a relationship in their imagination that far surpasses reality.

With the exception of the increasing reliance on 'crumb communication' (texts etc), the internet, and the prevalence of 'casual relationships,' such as booty calls and friends with benefits, the concept of fantasy relationships is nothing new. But in a world where many people dodge intimacy and commitment, while at the same time fearing being alone, plus the increasing obsession with not being 'rejected' and fear of making mistakes, it's never been so easy to end up in a fantasy relationship.

3

Fantasy relationships are what happen when you spend a disproportionate amount of time in your unconscious and not enough time in reality.

The Dreamer and the Fantasy Relationship is a companion guide to my book *Mr Unavailable and the Fallback Girl*, the definitive guide to understanding unavailable relationships. *Mr Unavailable and the Fallback Girl* is for every woman who has ever allowed a man to repeatedly default to her for a shag, an ego stroke, shoulder to lean on or any other fringe benefits he can enjoy without actually having to commit or even be emotionally, physically, or spiritually available. It's inspired by my personal experiences and the subsequent changes and realisations I went through to become emotionally available, as well as my observations of many relationships while I've been writing Baggage Reclaim.

In *Mr Unavailable and the Fallback Girl*, I explain the seven primary roles that women in these relationships take up: Yo-Yo Girl, Buffer, Other Woman, Florence Nightingale, Renovator, Flogger and Miss Independent/Miss Self-Sufficient. As a Fallback Girl, it's not unusual to have flitted back and forth between these roles over the course of your relationship history or even juggled two or more at a time. It's safe to say that there's a fantasy element to the relationships yielded from these roles, because of the betting on potential, cloaking in illusions and very rarely being in the present. However, I wanted to introduce a new role, the Dreamer, for if you've either engaged in these roles, but there's been a heavy element of virtual and imagination and not enough human interaction, or you've been burnt from being a Fallback Girl and have found yourself retreating from the real world and dating.

Mr Unavailable is rather handy. While he often has his 'good points' (while being thin on the ground on the things that add up to a mutual, healthy, fulfilling relationship, by being emotionally, physically, and spiritually distant), he's actually perfect for the Dreamer who wants to admire and love from a distance plus spend more time thinking about 'coulds' and 'shoulds' rather than actually making them happen. All his blowing hot and cold, and putting in just enough crumbs to keep you ticking over, leave you free to fill in the gaps with whatever the hell you like. After all, an available man wanting to put both of his feet into a relationship would expose you to too much 'risk' and reality.

Never has it been so easy to be fed on a diet of crumbs. When Mr Unavailable is a Shopper (the type that spends a lot of time online, hiding behind his phone and faux busy life) and collecting attention, he ends up being able to get a disproportionate level of interest from you, live off faux intimacy by bamboozling his way to 'instant intimacy', while often doing little more than being a pen pal with a side order of sweet nothings and 'sexts'.

The Dreamer and the Fantasy Relationship is aimed at every woman who is actively and persistently rejecting reality in favour for her unconscious and imagination. Whether it's that you get too carried away and find it difficult to differentiate between what's fake and what's real, or you've become so afraid and sensitive to the possibility of rejection, hurt, risk, or 'failure' that you're playing it safe in your imagination, this book serves as a reality check and wake up call.

Did you know that by being emotionally dishonest with yourself and partaking in the fantasy you're automatically unavailable for an available relationship?

This book isn't about the 'science' and 'psychology' behind fantasy relationships – I'm not a doctor or counsellor. I've deconstructed my own dodgy experiences and those of many others because, even though we are all unique, it's actually quite freaky how similar we can be when dealing with the same core issues. There are a *tonne* of books and journals out there that explore the science and psychology of relationships – my job is to inspire you to look at relationships and yourself with a fresh perspective and apply it. At the time of writing, Baggage Reclaim is read by over half a million people across the globe every month – all seeking to change their view of themselves and relationships. You can change yours too.

If you want to understand unavailable relationships and how they link to fearing commitment, abandonment, making mistakes, and the possibility of getting hurt again, I translate these experiences, behaviours and mindsets into relatable concepts that you can understand and apply to your own experiences, so that you can use them as a springboard to seek further help, for instance with a professional, or to begin taking action.

Any relationship, or even the prospect of one, where there was some level of emotional investment takes some time to get over, but it's safe to say that it can be awfully difficult to let go of a relationship that didn't actually exist or was as flimsy as a sandcastle built in the sky. What many people don't recognise about grieving the loss of relationships is that it's not just about when you break an actual relationship; it can also be about grieving the loss of hope and what you thought might be. When you're a Dreamer, you're not doing this and are, in fact, holding tight not only to the dream but a massive avoidance of rejection. Unfortunately, it's a vicious circle because the more you avoid your feelings, the more you remain in denial, the more unavailable you become, the greater the likelihood of either opening yourself up to pain with this Mr Unavailable, or finding fresh pain with a new one.

You're not alone, your habit isn't unique and there are very real reasons why you interact in your relationships in this way. While what you've been doing can feel like it's 'working' for you in the sense that you meet your objectives of 'loving' from a distance, avoiding action and dodging the things that you fear, it's not actually working in the wider sense. It's a very lonely existence no matter how good your imagination is and when you have someone who isn't fulfilling their 'role' in real life, it creates a great deal of anxiety, pain and rejection. Ironically, what you've failed to recognise in all this, is that you're rejecting 1) you, 2) trying for a healthy relationship in reality, and 3) participating in reality – this is more rejection than you'd ever experience if you were a fully accountable adult out in the real world.

It's time to come back to reality so that you can tackle and break a habit of avoidance and finally take steps to make changes in your life.

Until you address your Dreamer mode, you're unavailable for a healthy relationship, never mind being unavailable for a relationship in the real world full stop. There's more to life than what's going in your head.

QUICK RECAP: UNAVAILABLE RELATIONSHIPS

Being **emotionally unavailable** means not being fully emotionally present. It is struggling or being unable to access emotions healthily and, as a result, being emotionally distant due to 'walls' acting as barriers to true emotional intimacy. Fully experiencing all feelings, whether good, bad or indifferent, is avoided because they create vulnerability, so feelings are often experienced for a limited time and in bursts as opposed to on an ongoing basis. Emotional unavailability equates to intimacy issues – being afraid of the consequences of getting truly close to someone such that to lose them would hurt.

The vulnerabilities are protected by keeping people at a distance and/or being involved with similar people so that the risk is minimised. Via this safeguarding, being stretched emotionally or being available is avoided, and even when hurt or 'failure' at a relationship is experienced, it's not 'hurt hurt' or 'failure failure', because on a deeper level there is recognition that this wasn't going to work anyway and the emotional distance ensures the unavailable person was never truly in it. Being emotionally unavailable has a knock-on effect, so it also triggers physical unavailability such as disappearing, flaking out, not following through on promised action, or even avoiding sex.

Mr Unavailable is emotionally, physically and spiritually unavailable, while enjoying the fringe benefits of a relationship such as a shag, an ego stroke and shoulder to lean on, without truly committing to you. You know him well: ambiguous, tricky to read, blows hot and cold, backs off when you come too close, chases you when you cut him off, has a list of excuses as long as his arm, with actions rarely matching his words. He's probably the most popular man to date as he tends to straddle the fence between 'nice guy' and 'bad boy'. Only doing things on his terms, he's mastered the art of getting all the trappings of a relationship, often by creating the illusion of a promised loaf and chucking you crumbs of attention and affection instead. Put on a pedestal by every woman he becomes involved with, he throws out just enough promise to have you betting on potential but he perpetually disappoints. He's the man who doesn't commit – to you, to action, to his emotions – and as a result he's a limited man, with a limited capacity for commitment, creating limited relationships.

Mr Unavailable's inadvertently complicit partner is you, the **Fallback Girl**, the woman he habitually defaults to or 'falls back' on to have his needs met, while selling you short in the process. Accommodating his idiosyncrasies and fickle whims, you're ripe for a relationship with him because you are unavailable yourself (although you may not know it) and are slipping your own commitment issues in through the back door behind his. You get blinded by chemistry, sex, common interests and the promise of what he could be – if only he changed or you turned into The Perfect Woman. Too understanding and making far too many excuses for him, you have some habits and beliefs that are standing in the way of you having a mutually, fulfilling healthy relationship... with an available man. Pursuing or having a relationship with Mr Unavailable is symbolic of your need to learn to love yourself more and to set boundaries and raise standards.

Unavailable relationships arise when you have two people with emotional unavailability issues. There's always one, more powerful, party who dictates the relationship on their terms – *the driver* – and the other party who goes along with it – *the passenger*. The combination of Mr Unavailable and the Fallback Girl is what happens when you hide your often unknown unavailability issues behind his somewhat more obvious ones. You allow him to take you on a messy journey through an unavailable relationship.

The premise of a Mr Unavailable and the Fallback Girl relationship is actually quite simple. While we may not realise it, we all choose or align ourselves with people who reflect our beliefs. When they're unhealthy, whether it's because they're negative and/or unrealistic, unavailable relationships get created.

Beliefs are premises that we hold to be true and what we believe is often unconsciously reflected in our actions.

If we didn't do things in line with what we believe, we'd have to adapt our beliefs – this is avoided at all costs by an unavailable person, for fear of being vulnerable and having to get uncomfortable and, more importantly, take action. Each party ends up creating their own self-fulfilling prophecy, which is why, if you've had more than one of these relationships, it feels like you're on a very annoying merry-go-round.

If you've got a 'type' that's yet to yield you a happy, successful relationship, or have found yourself in a string of familiar situations that have you feeling bad about yourself, you're engaging in **Relationship Insanity** – carrying the same beliefs, baggage and behaviours; choosing same or similar guys; then expecting different results.

Those choices you're making are working in tandem with your conscious and unconscious beliefs to create a self-fulfilling prophecy that then reinforces those beliefs. What you believe about love, relationships or yourself is not necessarily true in the wider sense, but it is true in the context of your beliefs and engaging with Mr Unavailable. A different set of beliefs as reflected in your actions, along with changed habits, would create a whole other truth.

Being unavailable affects your ability to connect effectively and healthily with yourself and others. Combined with your background beliefs, it manifests itself in a variety of habits that perpetuate the unavailability by creating situations that allow you to remain unavailable. As a result when you have these issues it means you automatically have commitment issues.

Commitment resistance is actively, or in subtle, passive aggressive ways, resisting being absolute in binding yourself to another person. It's a fear of dealing with the vulnerability that comes with being responsible and accountable for one's self and others and it triggers resistance through literally avoiding and resisting commitment or sabotaging and stalling the processes that bring it about. Also commonly referred to as 'commitment-phobia', there are disproportionate fears and beliefs that prevent being able to fully commit. Emotional unavailability and commitment are intrinsically linked, because if you can't even commit to feeling out feelings, there certainly won't be a commitment to a relationship or definite outcomes. Whether it means putting both feet into the relationship, or opting out and staying out, the perpetual indecision and fear means living in limbo in an uncomfortable 'comfort' zone.

The easiest way to avoid commitment is to take refuge in a relationship where commitment is difficult because your partner shows or verbally communicates that they themselves don't want to put both of their feet in and commit. When faced with the decision of opting out, commitment-resisters flip-flap in indecision or keep going back to the relationship after it's ended. Failing that, the dominant party in the relationship can always blow hot and cold and pull a variety of manoeuvres to ensure that the show never really gets off the ground. Yep, that's what a typical relationship between Mr Unavailable and the Fallback Girl can look like.

You want to commit to those who don't want to commit and who actively resist commitment. When you're erring on the side of fantasy more than reality, you only want to commit when you know that there's shag all commitment on offer. This isn't the same as commitment.

Often we don't recognise that we resist or have a phobia of commitment because, unlike other phobias such as a fear of spiders, water, lack of space, people or buttons, there are no obvious signs of distress. When confronted with a man or the possibility of a relationship you aren't necessarily going to have an overt reaction and freak out, break out in a sweat, panic attack or run for the hills. You're also having relationships whereas you'd obviously avoid, for example, spider situations.

Instead, commitment resisters tend to engage in subtle and not-so-subtle, conscious and unconscious actions that sabotage opportunities, relationships and situations that may place them in the zone of having to realise the fear of committing. Often these actions are in direct conflict with aspirations and desires that are verbally expressed, or desired, but as with everything, actions do speak louder than words... or illusions.

FANTASY RELATIONSHIPS

EXPLORED

*There's no such thing as loving from a distance. There's admiring
from a distance, crushing from a distance, feeling moderate affection
from a distance, adoring, caring and being infatuated by, but if you
withhold yourself from experiencing true intimacy while cloaking
yourself in illusions, the one thing you're not doing is loving them
in a loving relationship, which means that you're not being loved in
a loving relationship either.*

An **illusion** is a false idea or belief, or a deceptive
appearance or impression.

A **fantasy** is an idea with no basis in reality – in
essence, your imagination unrestricted by reality.
Reality is the state of things as they exist. It's what
you see, hear, and experience.

A **fantasy relationship** is improbable or impossible.
This might be news to your ears if you steadfastly
believe that what you imagine is actually possible or
that the potential you envision for an illusion-filled

relationship is very possible, but the whole point of having a fantasy relationship is because it isn't real or it's not actually likely to become real, so you'll choose your 'marks' well.

When it's improbable, it may be that they're unavailable anyway – whether that's because they're emotionally unavailable, or because they're actually in a relationship with someone else and/or are emphatically stating that a relationship with you isn't going to happen. Or it becomes highly improbable from the moment that you lose track of who they actually are and attribute qualities, characteristics and values that they don't have, are betting on potential, or still clinging to the past. The further away from the truth of who they are, the greater rendering of impossibility. Of course, it will also be impossible if they're dead, a celebrity or a complete work of fiction.

Fantasy relationships are like a magical blend of your wishes – a combination of how you think things 'would' be or 'should' be, based on your conscious and unconscious beliefs (including some unhealthy and/or unrealistic ones). They cater to your self-fulfilling prophecy, because how you conduct yourself mentally ends up affecting your actions, so whatever negative effects you've predicted for the real world end up coming true.

In your fantasies, you're likely to be at your optimum, being who you only wish you could be in real life, which may be what you think 'wins' the 'perfect' person or reflects a person that experiences no problems. In fact, how you imagine yourself, means you're practically Teflon coated in your fantasies. Or, you may think you're 'exactly the same' as you are in real life (although you're unlikely to have a realistic perception of yourself), but your fantasy partner may be in possession of characteristics, qualities, and values that reflect the you that you'd like to be.

We're unconsciously attracted to people in possession of qualities we think we'd like to or ought to have. This can play itself out in the worst way within abusive relationships where, while their behaviour is awful and unacceptable, there may be a part of you that wishes that you could act out their level of aggression.

By 'engaging' in fantasy relationships, you're actively disconnecting from reality by persisting in dwelling at length on illusions. This makes you inactive in the real world. The difference between you and someone who is more realistic, is that they spend far shorter periods of time in their unconscious and can still clearly differentiate between reality and their imagination. In fact, they value reality, so even when they are caught short by misjudgements and their aspirations for someone or something that don't come to fruition, they don't reject it. Even if you are capable of differentiating between reality and your imagination, you are actively choosing to opt for what you know to actually be untrue – denial.

When you believe that it's hard to let go of your grand ideas and say stuff like, *'It feels like I was in love with an illusion,'* or *'I'm finding it really hard to move on and accept what has happened,'* you've got reconciliation issues. When faced with making fantasy and reality consistent with one another, so that you can accept the truth of what has happened/is happening, or what you feel, do, or are being, you opt for the illusions which suspends you in No Man's Land, while opening you up to problems in the real world.

IMAGINE AN EXISTENCE WITH...

NO RESPONSIBILITY.
NO ACCOUNTABILITY.
NO CONFLICT.
NO PROBLEMS.
NO REJECTION.
NO MISTAKES.
NO RISK.
NO FAILURE.
NO FEAR.

NO 'ABANDONMENT'.

NO DISAPPOINTMENT.

PERMANENT FLUFFY CLOUDS, JOY AND CUDDLES.

COMPLETE CONTROL OF EVERYTHING.

This would be a perfect existence, which doesn't exist... unless you're in a fantasy relationship. In reality, the very things you desire in a fantasy relationship, whether it's consciously or unconsciously, actually mean this:

No responsibility = No achievement, no stake in anything whether it's good, bad or indifferent, no remorse.

No accountability = No ownership, no honest account of your experiences, no growth.

No conflict = No voice, no resolution, no judgement (which may simply come down to judging the situation and making a decision), no growth.

No problems = No differentiation, no stretching, no opportunity to deal with a problem and be proud of having made yourself a part of the solution and come out the other side.

No rejection = No acceptance, no limits, no deciding what you say YES and NO to.

No mistakes = No feedback, no learning, no awareness.

No risk = No stretching, no gains, no pushing, no ambition, no trust, no common sense, no managed risks through intelligence, awareness, observation and action.

No failure = No success.

No fear = No drive, no ambition, no healthy fear, no vulnerability, no new experiences.

No 'abandonment' = No personal security or security with another discovered through mutual trust, no strength, no thriving and surviving, no being in control of whether you stay or leave.

No disappointment = No surprises, including the pleasant and wonderful ones.

Permanent fluffy clouds, joy, and cuddles = No contrast, no seasons, no down time to rise up again.

Complete control of everything = No one else has responsibility, accountability, or free will – it would just be you at the controls and dials. **Yep... it would all be on you.**

This right here is what fantasy relationships are about – avoidance of the 'bad', the pain, the discomfort, the uncomfortable unknown, and living in itself. The only thing is that you end up avoiding life itself, which means that you miss out on the wonderful aspects of life that come along with being present and accountable such as the good, the happiness, the comfort of real life and the opportunities.

Fantasy relationships and living your life unconsciously create very real problems in real life.

- You frustrate and disappoint those who care about you.
- You miss out.

Believing that you're loved, more successful, problem-free, responsibility-free, respected, cared etc, while living in a fantasy *is* an illusion.

Persisting in fantasy relationships is a search for perfection that doesn't exist. In real life, whoever you're involved with while being stuck on your fantasy will fall short. The truth is, most people struggle with 'failing' all the time and being berated, whether it's verbally or through your actions that reflect your dissatisfaction and lack of acceptance, for not living up to perfection. Of course, because perfection doesn't exist, it's like saying you can never be satisfied, whether it's by your own means, or by another person within a relationship.

'LIVING' A LIE

Any relationship based on illusions, fantasy, denial, rationalising, minimising, excuses and basically deception is a lie. Whether you're lying, they are or both of you are, it renders the relationship null and void.

You may think, 'Lie? I don't think they/I have been lying.'

A **lie** is a deliberately false statement.

There is a tendency for us to become preoccupied with 'intention' in relationships, but if your relationship and any perceptions you have about it is based on illusions, fantasy, denial and excuses, this whole situation is founded on a mistaken impression.

Intention is all about doing something with conscious purpose.

Many of us have 'good intentions', but you'll find that's all they'll remain if you're lacking action – which every person who engages in a fantasy relationship is. While there are many things you're doing that are a by-product of a habit of not living consciously, the one thing you do with conscious purpose is cling very hard to the illusions created by your fantasising and assuming.

Particularly after you recognise that one or both of you is lying and you don't seek to immediately rectify the situation by reconciling the lie with the truth, taking responsibility, and moving into a position of honesty – one that respects the truth – it's game over, no credits.

There's nowhere to go because lies on top of lies on top of more lies and beyond, just digs you further into the 'lie hole'. As it wasn't nipped in the bud so that your relationship could be put onto a level footing, neither of you can truly trust in yourselves or the other that the truth is now 'out there' between you and that you're not lying about the fact that you're now being honest, or even lying to yourselves. If you've ever been around someone who doesn't have a realistic vision of themselves, they can actually be very convinced of their own lies, so even if you decide to stick to facts, you'll become surplus to requirements because you're a reality check.

It's better to start fresh and accept no lies from yourself or others – then you know exactly where you are.

IS FANTASISING EVER HEALTHY?

Fantasies are useful for exploring ideas – a bit like a mental dummy run. They can enable you to tap into your creativity, examine who you are or ideas about what you want from yourself and your life in the future, sexual desires, and even to work through issues. Some of these may be things that you don't want to make into a reality – for example, you may have a fantasy of having a three-way but the idea of it may turn you on more than actually taking the actions to do so. Other fantasies, by helping you identify what may be unacknowledged desires and aspirations, can also help you to refocus your efforts, make small, medium or even big changes, and recognise areas of your life that are not satisfying you.

I fantasised about being self-employed, writing all the time, getting my ideas out there. I did the latter but, eventually, as I was being put in the position of making choices that turned me in a different direction from what I wanted, I had to put my proverbial money where my mouth was. I've now been self-employed, writing full-time and putting my ideas out there for nearly four years at the time of writing this. I'd fantasised for most of my life about feeling accepted, loved, empowered and being in a loving relationship – in real life, I had a string of relationships with unavailable men, one of whom even had a girlfriend. Again, I've had to walk the walk because it turned out that these ideas and desires were not things I wanted to leave in my unconscious while my real life resembled a motorway pile up. That fantasy has also become a reality –

I love and like myself and I'm in a loving relationship, which means I experience a great deal of happiness and satisfaction in my life, individually and within my relationship.

You'll notice that your fantasies have crossed into unhealthy when there's such a great disparity between your ideals and reality, that it leaves you hungry, frustrated, agitated, disappointed and even resentful. It's difficult to see when you're knee deep in it, but it's hard for those who are affected. I've seen people so caught up in their vision of what their ideal job or career looks like, that they made life very difficult for their colleagues. My own mother made her dissatisfaction that her family wasn't like the Brady Brunch clear. We hadn't met her fantasy of what family looked like and she often compared us to others – we just felt like major let downs and eventually came to recognise that we couldn't please her and that she was missing out.

I get it – real life sometimes isn't all that thrilling. I also understand that particularly when you've had a difficult childhood and have had to cope with painful experiences, often needing to fantasise for self-preservation, it's not uncommon to not only get used to this mode of being, but to have greater expectations and ideas about what can make you happy. That said, whether you've become this way as a child or an adult, these expectations about what your life 'should' and 'would' be, if only XYZ, can cause you to miss out on being an active part of your present, especially when you get trapped in inaction or feeling resentful of those around you. Life is sometimes a pain in the arse, miserable and bloody awful – it doesn't stay that way forever though, especially if you don't hold on to these feelings and stagnate in your life.

Having some fantasies can brighten up a day, remind you of your dreams and aspirations, and motivate you, but it's dicey territory when they disrespect your reality to the extent that you've taken your hands off the wheel of your life.

All of this fantasising is like pressing your face against the shop window of your own mind and torturing yourself about things you think you can't or won't have, even though it turns out that these things are available for free, with some healthy work that doesn't feel like 'work work'.

Don't get things twisted and think that daydreaming or having fantasies is a bad thing – it's not. However, there's daydreaming, then there's living in a dreamlike state, making decisions based around it without much thought for what's happening in reality. There's a reason it's called daydreaming – it's using your active state to be inactive by dreaming about what is likely to be a fantasy about happy stuff when you're awake, which distracts you from life. It's like life-jacking yourself – you can't make things happen and be in sniffing distance of a chance of it, if you're not in reality making it happen.

TYPES OF FANTASY RELATIONSHIP

Fantasy relationships can feature a real person that you're involved with, even if it's in a limited capacity, and can of course involve imaginary people – those who don't exist at all and are purely created from your imagination, and those who do exist but that you don't actually know/have zero involvement with. For the purpose of understanding fantasy relationships in the context of helping you further understand unavailable relationships, I focus on four main types and one 'surprise' secondary.

Virtual

Characterised by the majority of the interaction being online (email, instant messenger, Facebook, forums, blog comments, Twitter etc), and/or by text, although it's not unheard of for phone to be involved, especially in intense bursts, these involvements give an illusion of a greater connection and involvement than actually exists. This is caused by disproportionate feelings and perceptions of what you think is happening and what will happen, that outpace any real action, including physical interaction.

They tend to either be very intense at the beginning and possibly for a few months then fizzle out, often when real life is 'interrupting', or operate in fits and bursts over an extended period of time. Alarmingly, while the 'chatter' can be love letters (or messages) proclaiming feelings and intentions, it's not unusual for the contact to be filled with weather, work, 'How are you?', sports, and other innocuous chit chat contrasted at times by very sexual talk and images. In talking with many readers, it seems that there is a general misguided assumption that people don't correspond in this manner and reach out to you, particularly over an extended period of time, unless there are serious romantic feelings and intentions. You may find that the speed at which the intensity and tone of the contact changed is, in retrospect, rather alarming. Of course, these involvements largely remain feelings, plans that don't come to fruition and chit chat, which invariably becomes frustrating when looking for real commitment, or even basic action.

Virtual 'relationships' serve as a distraction from real life for both parties, plus they're in effect recreational – they're means of passing time that give an inaccurate impression of busyness. That said, it's not uncommon to find oneself at a loss when things fizzle out or come to an end, with some people feeling like they almost have an addiction to being in contact. The true test of the 'reality' of these involvements is whether you can pick up the phone and see them without obstacle... or do you have to make excuses for why it's not possible?

One of the pitfalls of virtual involvements is that you end up thinking that there's no way that someone would say or write the things they do if they didn't feel the same way. Unfortunately, they may be thinking that there's no way that someone would actually believe that there's a 'proper' relationship based on texts, emails and anything else that dominates a primarily virtual interaction.

Crushes

While this can involve you admiring them from a distance and having very little, if any, contact, this is actually likely to be a situation where you're making a lot out of limited involvement. They don't see you in 'that way', or may be completely unaware of your interest. It's not unusual to actually enjoy the feeling of being infatuated more than trying to make a relationship happen – there may be no genuine desire to act upon your feelings. These situations inspire fascination, admiration, wonderment, obsession, jealousy, possessiveness and, in dark moments, complete despair. As reality doesn't intervene quickly enough, the object of your affections ends up on a pedestal that leaves you hovering below, which only serves to exacerbate the feeling of rejection you seek to avoid, and may even have you feeling inferior.

There's a lot of seeing meaning where there is no meaning, plus, even when you pick up 'negative signals' that impede on your fantasy, the 'great' thing about crushes is that you can spin them into anything that suits. When enveloped in your feelings, you believe that they feel the same way as you – it's just that circumstances beyond your control are conspiring against you both and keeping a 'great love' from happening. While these are often characterised by being short-term in nature, they can go on for several months, a year, or even a few years. These experiences only serve to highlight that being 'in love' is something that you can do on your own, but it's not a loving relationship if the two of you are not together in a mutual relationship.

The longer a crush continues for, the more improbable and, in fact, impossible, that you being with that person becomes. Aside from the fact that crushes are equivalent to putting someone through an exaggerator machine, if you were to ever act upon your feelings and have an opportunity to be involved with them, they'll 'ruin' it by not living up

23

to your expectations, or by turning out to be exactly like the type of person that you
don't want.

Projection Projects

While you're involved with someone in real life, who you see them as is actually a mental image. These relationships are characterised by too many illusions, denial and, in actual fact, bullshit. You may go into these situations with your vision of how you think a relationship 'should' be and then slot them in, or meet them, take a few isolated characteristics, qualities and values that may even contradict one another, then over-correlate them and assume they must be your perfect match and in possession of other things you deem attractive, or you may even take random, unrelated and unimportant things and see potential.

It is not unusual for you to initially feel like the more powerful party in the relationship – 'the driver' – and then experience immense confusion when the whole bait and switch happens, where suddenly a relationship that you felt very in control of, and even a little superior in, has you chasing them and having to fight hard for every crumb. The projection project is most likely to involve someone you feel is lacking in certain areas that if they fulfilled your fantasy would make them a better person.

These are frustrating relationships for both parties – you, because you'll be pissed off that they fail to meet your vision of things, and them, because you're actually relating with a false image of them, not them, which is actually quite disrespectful and rejects them. This type of fantasy relationship has its part in many an unavailable relationship and, if you're guilty of treating partners like a blank canvas on which to paint your image of them, your great expectations and over-active imagination are your troublesome 'brushes'.

Sadly, by making your relationships Projection Projects, you either miss out on someone who is actually better in reality than whatever you're imagining, or you let someone who already isn't a healthy relationship partner hide their light under your illusion bushel, giving them an opt-out on responsibility and accountability.

Orbiters

Like taking a mental vacation to your 'ideal relationship', these 'involvements' aren't designed to ever 'land' in the real world. It may include fantasising about a celebrity or deciding that the only person who is the right match for you is someone that's dead and possibly famous. Or they just don't exist.

This type of fantasy relationship is included because it makes you unavailable for an available relationship in the real world. If you're single, being heavily invested in this type of fantasy will prevent you from forging real connections because you're in essence emotionally removing yourself from the market for a relationship that cannot and isn't happening, plus it creates very unrealistic expectations of yourself, others and what the dating pool should deliver for you. It may be tempting to retreat to this fantasy if you've been single for so long after a serious heartbreak, that you just don't want to 'run this risk' again.

If you're in a relationship, you'll exert undue pressure on it and actually exclude your partner by being unavailable due to your investment in the fantasy, because it will begin to impact on your behaviour, even though you may not realise it. It's actually not too dissimilar to emotional cheating and, as you're so 'out of it', you will fail to recognise how your behaviour is impacting on your relationship. Orbiters are a major distraction and are the safest place for someone who is extremely hurt and trying to avoid any 'new' pain.

The remarkable thing about Orbiters is that it's like telling yourself that no one, out of near 7 billion people on the planet, has the capability of being in a mutually fulfilling relationship with you. This means, after all the effort you go to to avoid rejection, hurt, disappointment etc, you deal yourself the biggest blow because, with your thinking, the fundamental message communicated is that nobody can love you.

Affairs

I couldn't write about fantasy relationships without including affairs, involvements with people who are already in a relationship with someone else, or lying to and dishonouring your commitment to a current partner. They're included as a fantasy relationship, albeit a secondary one, because, really, it's like play acting at a relationship, cherry picking the convenient bits, avoiding the unpleasant parts and essentially getting all the fringe benefits without the responsibility, conflict, commitment etc – the best of both worlds.

While some affairs are short-lived and were never about going beyond a fling, many revolve around a fantasy that the other party is going to leave and make good on their promises (or hints) one day. Cheaters have this fantasy that if the other party was that special, they'd leave, or that if their current partner was that special they wouldn't cheat, which is bullshit.

The big fantasy in affairs though is this: you think you can't be 'left left', 'abandoned abandoned', 'rejected rejected', or 'hurt hurt', because he's already unavailable and a relationship in the fullest sense doesn't exist.

If you're the one who's cheating, when the affair is going well, you have that fantasy of no conflict, problems, rejection, etc. You also believe that you can't technically be responsible for a relationship based on lies, especially when you technically have responsibilities elsewhere, so you have the illusion of being guilt free with 'justifiable' actions.

Of course, by participating in what can be a top secret affair, you're unavailable for an available relationship. If you're the one who's cheating, you're unavailable to your partner because you're too busy exploring other options. You're also unavailable to reality.

Affairs involve an incredible amount of deception on both sides – there's no such thing as an honest cheat and, unfortunately, if you're the Other Woman, you end up deviating from your own moral compass, listening to lies, lying to yourself and to others, which can be isolating. Beginning under all sorts of circumstances, affairs can gradually creep up on you as a friendship starts to take on an undertone which fuels the imagination, or the result of a drunken evening after work that then gets repeated, or having the attached Returning Childhood Sweetheart get in touch to wax lyrical about old times. It's this fantasy that something great will come out of deceit.

The fantasy can get out of hand if it was intended to be a fling and, as the Other Woman, you read more into it and run away with this fantasy that it means so much more and that you're going to be together. Depending on how they handle it, they may try to let you down gently, which will give you the wrong idea and likely convince you that there's a chance, or they'll put you straight and you'll feel rejected and possibly very angry. It's not unheard of for an affair to lapse into being more like a virtual relationship – while it may start out this way, it's often the case that in an effort to water things down and let you down gently, they keep up varying levels of contact. They may feel like they're not even in an affair anymore because it's just texts, email and the occasional bit of sexting. You'll be particularly primed for this if you're avoiding something painful in your life such as a divorce – you'll be satisfied by the crumbs... until you want more.

The trouble with affairs is that there is this misconception that the very existence of the affair is based on there being such a depth of feeling, attraction and desire to leave that the person cheating is willing to risk their existing relationship. When the chips are down, this is the illusion you'll keep returning to. Unfortunately, cheaters operate on managed risk – they'll cross that bridge when they come to it, so they're not taking as big a risk as you imagine.

If you're cheating, you immediately get a sense of how you handle problems and uncomfortable feelings – by avoiding them in a fantasy. If you're the Other Woman, you can immediately learn that you have hit a personal low and are taking refuge in a faux relationship.

FANTASY RELATIONSHIPS ARE ONE-SIDED.

You vs fantasy.
You vs unreciprocated.
You vs your partner and the fantasy.

You are placing yourself outside of reality, hence you cannot be available for a relationship or even the love, attention, respect, care, trust, sex, comfort, contact and anything else you profess to want.

By being embedded in a fantasy, you exclude yourself from real life, which can be isolating and lonely, or give off the wrong vibes to those around you.

Hankering for someone who doesn't reciprocate excludes you from the 'available' pool. By focusing your efforts on an unreciprocated affection, aside from wallowing in rejection, it also opts you out of availability for an available relationship with a reciprocating party.

The expectations that arise from your fantasy when you're in a relationship actually exclude you and your partner from a real relationship.

HELLO DREAMER

If you have a tendency to have crushes, get lost in your feelings, continue feeling even when it becomes clear it's not reciprocated, or can weave a fantasy relationship out of words and your imagination, you're a **Dreamer**. Carrying a huge fear of intimacy, you find it safer to live in your mental world rather than risk a 'real' rejection. While all Fallback Girls have avoidance issues and are chasing a feeling, you don't truly want to get close to anyone – you want that 'feeling' from a distance. Your mind is very rarely in the present, you're very 'dreamy' and have often been doing your imaginary world thing for a long time, possibly since childhood, or after you experienced a traumatic event. It may be a learned coping mechanism for shutting out anything 'unpleasant' that's eating up too much reality and causing you to feel vulnerable. Often, all you need is a little attention or for him to be in possession of a couple of characteristics or qualities that you overvalue, for you to create a connection that ignites your imagination.

If you're entirely honest with yourself, which may be difficult when you're prone to fantasy, you feel much more secure and in control in your illusionary world than you do in real life. I've read enough emails and comments from Fallback Girls to know that sometimes you can become so overwhelmed by your experiences and the pain, and lose so much confidence in yourself that you feel helpless to deal with a real relationship and take comfort in your imagination where everything feels and looks a lot better.

Unfortunately, in real life, you're still a Fallback Girl and, while you're immersed in your feelings and imagination, you miss out on obvious signs that all is not well. You don't register that you're not being 'matched', that they've left the building or were never even there, or that who you think they are is not actually who you're involved with. This 'loving' and 'trusting' blindly opens you up to, at best, being taken advantage of and, at worst, being abused if you're involved with someone. If you're not, it can cause you to become very numb and struggle to discern fiction from reality. On top of this, you lose significant chunks of your life.

Dreamer Characteristics

Afraid of abandonment, intimacy, conflict, and rejection.

May not realise you have perfection issues.

Detail-driven imagination but often quite vague in reality. May get obsessed with detail also.

Lonely. Although you may have friends, you're likely to lack close friendships.

Prone to long distance and virtual relationships.

Tend to be involved in situations that are a 'long shot'.

Co-dependent – without the fantasy you lose all sense of your identity.

Identify with fairy tales.

Not hot on being responsible and accountable for yourself and your experiences.

Think you 'interact' with many others, but often, in reality, you don't.

Say stuff like, 'I've really tried to meet someone,' or 'Nobody has approached me.' Even though you aren't social, you're immersed in your bubble, may be emotionally invested in someone else, and you're unavailable!

Likely to be a heavy computer, internet and text user, which may include keeping track of them on social networking sites.

Very routine – gym, work, supermarket, gym, work, supermarket, gym, work, supermarket, do same old social thing, gym, work, supermarket and lather, rinse, repeat.

Use fantasy to feel more confident – the lack of confidence may be caused by abuse in childhood, being bullied, over sheltered or feeling unloved.

Distinctly unwilling to take a chance on love again. Think the 'right' person will jolt you out of your fantasy and 'make' you want to try again.

Deeply hurt by one particular breakup or deeply traumatised by one particular experience.

Always on the lookout for 'signs' in the media or from peers and family to legitimise your thinking and behaviour – you read an article about singles or dating statistics and plunge into a downward spiral.

May have been diagnosed with Post Traumatic Stress Disorder (PTSD) or treated for depression or anxiety.

Living in the past and trying to right the wrongs of it through your fantasies.

Consider yourself to be more sensitive to experiences than other people – 'everyone else' is much stronger or hasn't had the same experiences as you that you believe legitimise your sensitivity.

Highly likely to be swept up in someone else's Fast Forwarding – when you're sped through the early stages of the relationship and miss crucial signs that all is not well.

Highly likely to be guilty of your own Fast Forwarding, pushing for them to declare feelings etc.

When you do get involved with someone, you privately have anxieties and concerns quite quickly after the initial bubble.

Bury your head in the sand about problems and signs that a relationship is unhealthy.

May be married or in a relationship but avoiding problems with an 'affair', typically an emotional one.

Major ruminator – just don't stop thinking and obsessing and thinking some more.

Keeping in touch with an attached 'friend' and ruminating over why they haven't 'chosen' you.

Believe you know people more than you do – may cross boundaries.

Make some of the most ridiculous assumptions as well as broad, sweeping generalisations.

Prescriber – have a fantasy ideal that you project onto real partners and expect them to fulfil unrealistic expectations.

Scared of mistakes so fantasise fixes or magically erase away problems.

Bargainer – extended mental conversations with a higher power or yourself trying to trade on what you can do next to keep the fantasy or 'win' him.

May believe you're in a relationship with someone who's just a friend or doesn't even know you exist.

Can get defensive or even aggressive when your 'truth' is challenged.

Coasted at school, university, work etc.

Absent minded and easily distracted – may find it difficult to focus.

Very creative although you may not actually use it productively.

Rigid ideas about what you need in a partner.

May have little or no relationship experience, but may have had many casual encounters.

Been accused of stalking, doing something vengeful, or had someone do No Contact on you.

May even have had run-in's with the law.

Blame everyone else and may assume victim status.

Talk the talk with the likes of a therapist and give a sense of false confidence, knowledge, and awareness.

May have a porn habit, possibly into some very hardcore stuff which may let you play out a more aggressive or assertive side of you.

Given to a lot of introspection – you just don't convert it into positive, productive insight.

Don't believe in yourself enough – it's like you're afraid of being in something real for long enough that they'd discover you're not as great as you actually are.

THE DREAMERS

Escapists

Possibly been escaping your life and your thoughts for as long as you can remember.

Know actions are destructive but feel 'powerless' to stop.

Not a problem solver.

May suddenly look up from a fantasy involvement and realise that your kids have changed dramatically.

Coaster and very distracted – have likely chosen a relationship and career that makes it 'easier' to mentally check out.

Likely to engage in emotional cheating – gives illusion of not having cheated.

May be into collecting attention.

May have experienced abuse or at the very least witnessed it as a child.

Have what appears to be a great life but feel very dissatisfied.

Life feels boring and overwhelming – seek fun by fantasising about someone else.

Area of your life feels very out of control.

Absent-minded from a real relationship, albeit unlikely to be a good one, he's just a 'prop' to the stage that's your imagination and expectations. While like Florences and Renovators (Fallback Girls that love trying to fix/heal/help or change Mr Unavailables) you may push for changes, you're happy to crack on with your imaginary scalpel in La La Land and live there instead.

While you may start out as the more powerful party in this

dynamic, aside from your fantasising making you automatically unavailable, you tend to have pseudo power in your relationships and end up revolving around on his terms especially when he stops doing things as you'd expect and you become more passive to maintain the Status Quo – being able to escape to your fantasies but not actually having to do anything. As he is a prop and you essentially just want to be free to let your imagination run riot, the last thing you need is him interrupting your reverie by exiting the relationship or playing up. Often, without you realising it, you subtly adjust your behaviour to protect your 'interests'.

Your dreamy ways will seem charming, sexy and even flattering initially, but after a while they exert a lot of pressure, while at the same time you either become very frustrated and/or retreat further into your world. You have no genuine interest in resolving problems, engaging and basically being emotionally present, and, as a result, despite proclaiming how much you want to feel and do certain things, the limited connection in your relationship is further eroded.

You're resentful, angry, frustrated and disappointed in your current partner for 'failing' to meet unrealistic and unhealthy expectations that you've often not even communicated, and are creating a world that they cannot live up to.

When reality bites too much, you'll desperately avoid ending things – you could continue as you are forever, even though you may have said differently. At this point, you may blow very hot into the relationship, or appear to make greater efforts to resolve the issues, but when it all starts to require more effort and vulnerability, you back off into your little world again. You may find that you're able to Future Fake with the best of them, convincing him and possibly others of what you're going to be and do, and then doing the proverbial whistle and look in the other direction when it's time to deliver. Or blaming them for you not delivering – you'll be familiar with this if you've been on the receiving end of it with Mr Unavailable.

He'll likely be the one to end it, you'll be devastated that it didn't work out, go off into a dream world to cope, and then start another fantasy relationship with another Mr Unavailable who shows very little willingness or capacity to be a prop although he'll happily type words and chat, then give you the runaround.

You're also a prime candidate for cheating and will likely go after an ex who thinks the sun shines out of you, or someone doe-eyed and adoring, such as a work colleague who's bought into this idea that you're the victim of a poor partner and situation after you've told them about your dissatisfaction with your life. You'll talk like you really want to change your life and be with them, but you like the fantasy of it and the knowledge of them being 'there', more than the reality of having to take action and leave. In fact, if the affair is discovered, you'll fight tooth and nail to hold onto your partner but still try to keep the other party on the backburner, although it's not unknown for you to cut them off if they start intervening on your fantasy and bringing up uncomfortable feelings. That said, if the other party does things on your terms, you could keep the situation going forever, but if it doesn't work out, you'll likely start a new affair.

One tricky issue that can arise if you do have a 'secret affair' is that the other party may get tired of you not leaving your partner, which you may be afraid of doing because you don't want to run the risk of 'getting it wrong', or having to actually work at a 'proper' relationship and see if your long shot fantasy can come true. On them leaving, you may then feel compelled to finally 'leave' your relationship, only to then find yourself as the Other Woman. You'll then be angry with them and yourself, believing that had you acted sooner you could have had the fantasy and you may try to continue resolving the situation with him. What you don't do is resolve the problems that you're avoiding – the relationship that you've been cheating on and the feelings and issues within you that you're avoiding, which means you never really gain the lesson and the growth out of this.

Crushers

More hurt than you've admitted by a breakup.

Feel bad for secretly being afraid of trying again at a relationship, so instead date people, but never progress things due to being 'in love' with the object of your crush.

Listen to conjecture from friends and colleagues – only takes one comment about how well you get on, to start a crush.

Likely to be a work colleague, a friend that you get on very well with or even neighbour.

Unable to work out if they're interested – it's very ambiguous.

Waiting for them to ask you out... but also afraid of it going wrong if they do.

Idolise them – they're on a major pedestal.

Likely crushed on bosses, teachers, professors or even your friends partners.

May enjoy talking about why he hasn't asked you out and what he might feel with your friends.

Preferring to admire and be admired from a distance, you're about unreciprocated love. Fearing obliterating the fantasy by making your true feelings known, either nothing happens between you but you may hang around, or you get involved in something ambiguous that your feelings stretch far beyond. Admiring and being admired from a distance also stops them from getting close enough that they may discover the 'flaws' you're afraid will stand between you and your happiness in a relationship. Eager for a diversion from a rejection or old hurts, you become attracted and deeply infatuated and then get overwhelmed by your feelings and lost in your imagination.

Crushes can also become quite attractive when you're transitioning after a major breakup, separation, divorce, or bereavement. It can seem quite scary to put yourself out there again and the object of your crush becomes someone who you get on very well with, they've been helpful, supportive etc. They then become this legitimate reason for why you're not moving your life forward or interested in someone else you've been dating – you don't want to put the kibosh on the possibility of you being together. At the same time, you may be afraid of ruining the friendship while fantasising that it's fear of losing you as a friend and not wanting to hurt you that's prevented them from asking you out. You might even blame the bad timing of their current partner and have a fantasy that's akin to a chick lit plot or romantic comedy film.

Of course, several months, a year, or even a few, go by and you still haven't been 'noticed' and you may begin to wonder what's wrong with you. You may even have managed to kiss or sleep together, but nothing has happened and, instead of taking the hint, you remain invested in the fantasy or even become frustrated with them. You basically keep waiting and the fall back to reality, especially if they move on with someone else, can be devastating, especially as it can feel like you've 'wasted' your time. Be careful as this is when you're most likely to throw yourself into an unhealthy relationship with someone else or even offer yourself up as the Other Woman to him.

When you're lonely and have a deep sense of self-loathing, the fantasy of your crush fills the voids, making you confident, more attractive and in control, and everything is perfect. Likely to latch onto a piece of information that fuels your fantasy ('I've been having a tough time with my girlfriend/she doesn't understand me'), you become unable to distinguish between your respective feelings, which means you may do things that you later come to view as being, at best, embarrassing and, at worst, humiliating, which of course will make you feel worse about yourself.

Likely used to very little affection, you will need very little interaction from him. However your fantasy may give you a sense of possession that doesn't match with reality and when his lack of interest or another relationship becomes apparent, you may attempt to control his agenda, voicing your displeasure and acting strangely around him, which may lead to you crossing boundaries. When conflict arises, it will fuel the sense of rejection and cater to your self-fulfilling prophecy of not being good and loveable enough. Trapped in the feelings of rejection which you mistake as 'love', you'll continue with the fantasy and may periodically try to gain attention. This will hurt very badly, especially when he moves on, or even becomes mean towards you.

Virtuals

Genuinely believe that texts, email etc, without regular human interaction is a relationship.
Or believe that sex with primarily virtual contact is a relationship.
Transitioning following a breakup, separation, divorce or bereavement.
Easier to hide this side of your life from friends and family and appear 'normal'.
Intimacy issues – love lazy communication as it keeps you distant and safe.
Used to little affection and interaction, so can do this for years.
May feel a compulsive need to send texts, emails etc.
Highly likely to cheat, even if it's 'just' emotional and fantasy.
May engage in a lot of sexual activity with several different people but still feel entitled to be treated like a girlfriend.
Very low feelings of self-worth, especially if experienced abuse and neglect as a child or parent was an addict.

Avoiding putting yourself out there in the real world, often deeming dating as scary, or online dating as 'necessary', via your computer you can get attention, have conversations, or even start a relationship, often feeling far more confident, expressive and in control. You're likely lonelier than you'd admit, eager for companionship and, in a world where people can paint a picture of themselves with words, no matter how inaccurate, you can feel like you've found a soul mate.

You are too reliant on distant and what can be lazy forms of communication. When it comes to texts, email, Facebook et al, you don't realise that you read them in the way that you'd like them to mean, which is perfect for someone with a predilection for fantasising. You'll come up with all sorts of reasons why you engage in these means of communication, but the truth is that it protects you from having to actually take action and engage at a more vulnerable level.

Likely avoiding old hurts, you might also be an ex-Crusher playing it safe. When you meet someone who seems to say all the right things and be and do exactly as you want, albeit virtually, your imagination runs wild. Latching onto pieces of information and over-correlating them, you love 'connections' and are a Fast Forwarder too, so want to be swept into his fantasy or sweep him into yours. You're also a prime candidate for getting involved in an affair, particularly with a married ex, old friend or your boss.

When you suggest plans, talk about the future, and share your passions and interests with him, he may initially play along, but, being a typical Mr Unavailable, he may feel hemmed in, especially if your expectations grow and you start attempting to translate them to the real world or appear to be trying to control his agenda. When he starts blowing hot and cold or disappears, you may shut it out, come up with excuses for him or even berate yourself. Attempts to make contact/track him down may follow and, if you're met with conflict or silence, you may become very angry or bombard him with attention, which will only fuel your sense of rejection and even self-loathing. Eventually you'll move on and lather, rinse, repeat.

The other dubious, and rather prevalent, form of virtual relationship is a casual sex involvement that's punctuated with texts, emails etc. You take the sex and nuggets of attention and inflate it into a 'relationship' that isn't reflective of your involvement. You begin to have needs, expectations, wants and a sense of entitlement that may cause you to feel territorial, possessive and even out of control.

You make a dangerous correlation between sexual involvement and their feelings/your feelings, or what you feel it entitles you to in relationship terms. These activities mean something to you and when it appears that they don't to him, it's a hard dose of reality that will leave you feeling rejected and eager to avoid the feeling, which means you will either indulge the fantasy further or find a new source of attention.

It's also not unheard of for Virtuals to be having sexual interactions both on and offline with several people, but to then become fixated on the one who doesn't jump to your beat. You may even be a hop, skip and jump away from being told you have a sex addiction, which may come to a head when you hit a very painful low and are forced to face your problems.

Tabbers

Extremely important to have the illusion of being in control.

Feeling very dejected and rejected.

Cannot see past your feelings.

Think a lot about what you're 'owed'.

Believe there are very good reasons for violating privacy.

May exploit work privileges to gain access to confidential information.

Spend a lot of time keeping track of their activity on Facebook... or asking friends to do it on your behalf.

May actually be cheating on a current partner and avoiding dealing with the problems in that relationship.

Contemplating accepting the loss or lack of interest resurrects a very painful old wound.

May feel paralysed by your 'need' to play detective, losing hours of your life investigating.

Have had an ex do No Contact because you wouldn't accept that it was over.

Threatened with a restraining order.

Possibly blocked or threatened with it on social media and/or phone.

You have a past of sorts with your Mr Unavailable – he might be an ex or a past interest that didn't reciprocate and you haven't accepted that the relationship or the hopes are over. What he likely doesn't know is that, while smarting from the rejection, you're keeping tabs on him and basically conducting your 'relationship' from a distance. For you, this relationship isn't over, possibly until you say it's over or something terribly humiliating happens that gives you a wake-up call, such as the po-po knocking on your door.

From stalking his Facebook page, checking his status updates, who has left comments and going through his photos, to checking dating sites to see if he's logged in and near losing your mind when he has, to following him on Twitter and agonising when he tweets with another woman, to logging into emails and voicemails, to watching outside his home, it's like voyeuristic punishment. You are tormenting yourself. You've failed to realise that you'd have gotten over this 'rejection' far sooner if you were not trapping yourself in a prison of your own making!

You're trying to control his agenda as a way of avoiding dealing with the rejection and knowing what he's doing gives you the illusion of being in control and stems your feelings of rejection. Of course, when he deviates from your view of things, the very feelings that you're trying to avoid will return full force.

It can all start innocently enough – you just want to see how he's been doing because you miss talking to him, or you've been panicking about him already moving on so you want to make sure he hasn't, or that if he has, it doesn't sound like he's 'changed'. Maybe you were suspicious that he was cheating on you or that you were thwarted by another interested party, so you just want to make sure that he hasn't and that you haven't made an error in judgement. It's only harmless, you think, only you feel compelled to check as soon as you wake and before you go to sleep. Sometimes you look up and realise that several hours have passed while you've been trawling photos, following the trail of friends, or ransacking his email. It's not unheard of for you to create a fake profile to flirt with him on a dating site and basically, it crosses from being something fairly innocuous that most would realise was inappropriate very quickly, into what feels like a compulsion.

Of course when he moves on or you get indicators that he might be, you may spiral into a panic, make contact with him, or even bombard him with attention and demands, which will only alienate you further. You may tell him about himself to his face, or via text/email, possibly revealing information that you could only have got by checking up on him. Depending on the level of engagement, you or he may engage in blocking one another on social media and then demanding to unblock.

Sometimes you use the information to sense when he may be vulnerable and likely to respond to your invitation to hang out. After sex or whatever, he goes back to being his usual self or assumes that was it and continues on his merry way.

This can cross into stalking/revenge territory and, if it gets this far, it can have serious consequences for your emotional health, as well as your professional and social standing. Hopefully this is the point where you will get help, but in the worst instances, feeling like your actions have cost you everything may give you a nothing-to-lose mentality.

It's easy to see why these situations don't seem 'that bad' initially because, pre-internet, if you wanted to keep tabs on someone, which is actually stalking, you'd have to make a hell of a lot more effort that involves sitting outside their home in your car, turning up at work, and making a general nuisance out of yourself... all of which I hope you're not doing alongside the whole tracking them on the internet thing...

This is very serious behaviour and whatever point that you realise that you're engaging in this is the point where you need to seek help. Trust me, you are not the first person to poke around in an ex's life online (it's an ad hoc pastime for millions of people and a lot of what Facebook et al are about), but there's curiosity that has no impact on your emotional well-being or your life, and then there's compulsively looking them up to give yourself an illusion of feeling in control.

After talking with many readers who have been in this situation, or at least flirted with it before recognising that it was getting out of hand, it's very likely that there is another relationship in your past that you haven't come to terms with so this ex that you're keeping tabs on is a way of avoiding that feeling of failure again. You've made a judgement about yourself, deeming you a 'failure' and a blanket feeling of control makes it feel like you have some sort of upper hand.

I've also found that if you have a current relationship where you feel like a failure and have been mistreated, then you may have sought solace or attention in an affair or flirtation which may have backfired. As you're avoiding the current relationship where you're pretty much at a stalemate with yourself because you feel like you 'can't' leave, when this affair or flirtation also doesn't work, it compounds the sense of failure so you feel compelled to keep an eye on them with the hopes of finding an 'angle' that can help you 'win' them and avoid failure, or the very nature of 'tabbing' actually gives you a purpose that consumes and distracts you from yourself and the relationship you're avoiding. Whatever you do, what you must do next is seek the help that you need so that options open up for you.

THE SHOPPER

In theory, you can become involved with any Mr Unavailable including in particular Transitionals (basically not over their ex or transitioning out of an old relationship), Cheaters (physically and/or emotionally playing hooky on an existing commitment), and Opportunists (users), but particularly in these modern times, you're most likely to be caught out with the **Shopper**.

Fond of collecting attention, he's highly likely to be found online or hiding behind his phone, plus may be partial to one-night stands, flings and short romances, both on and offline, and may even be juggling a few women at the same time. Like all Mr Unavailables, he's an intimacy dodger and likes to keep himself as distant as possible, so fuelling most of the communication through words and never meeting you, or only doing so very occasionally, coming up with the most absurd reasons for why it hasn't happened yet, or speeding you through a whirlwind, are high on his agenda. He's a dreamer himself, but is often more conscious of it due to him having the upper hand in the relationship, but wouldn't take any responsibility for any promises made off the back of the dreaming. He's the type that 'fishes' with ambiguous texts, leaves you waiting on Skype, asks you to transfer some money to him after

44

you've only known him for a month because his sister has been in an 'accident', gives you the best date or week of your life and is never heard from again, or has you waiting in every night for a call at a certain time while he's off pestering someone else or feathering his nest elsewhere.

Hard as it may be to hear, you have to recognise that it's the fact that you're so detached from the present that makes you attractive to Mr Unavailable. This isn't to say that he's not attracted to you, but the fact that you have a very different view to reality allows him to become very secure in the knowledge that he doesn't have to 'stump up'. He will recognise that you're an ideal 'mark' for his shenanigans because:

1) You tend to blow smoke up his arse, making him out to have qualities, characteristics and values that he doesn't, or exaggerating the crap out them. You pump him up and he actually doesn't have to do very much to win your attentions, affections and illusions which has him thinking that he's more special and valuable than he actually is.
2) When you talk about the relationship to him, it sounds like an entirely different one.
3) He's said stuff like, 'I'm not over my ex', 'I'm not looking for a relationship right now', 'I don't see you in that way' and other such guff and you're still there or hovering around, making out like you have a grand love together.
4) Your expectations of him and the relationship far surpass the reality of it.
5) You actually expect from him. Little do you realise, he has, at the very least, subtly, if not directly, been conveying that he's not reliable, consistent, committed, there or even interested.
6) Although you may see yourself very differently, the reality is that you're not producing the actions or even the mindset that reflects all of these

expectations. Let's be real, neither is he but he recognises that you're like two peas in an unrealistic pod.

Whether it's you thinking about your life together or making out that his feeble texts are like a goldmine of contact, or him seeming to think that he's owed a perfect woman in spite of the fact that he's unavailable and far from perfect himself, you're both inactive and unrealistic.

This is one of those situations where it might be all you, but if there's a Mr Unavailable in the equation, then someone is benefiting from your fantasy ways. That doesn't remove your accountability, but it's important to get back to base here: You're a Fallback Girl that chooses people that reflect your beliefs and that allow you to remain in your comfort zone. While your fantasies and any involvements may have involved some Mr Availables, it's more likely that they didn't, because an available man poses a risk of vulnerability and intimacy which you're trying to avoid, so you'll choose your 'marks' well because they'll be attached, immersed in their own problems or sitting at the end of a computer. Of course, as is always the case with unavailable relationships, eventually reality pierces the illusion bubble and much pain results.

Guys like the Shopper can toss you some words and some pipe dreams in crumb rations and sustain this flimsy relationship for years. While he may not be aware of your dreamy tendencies at the outset, when it becomes clear you're in LaLa Land and it doesn't set off alarm bells for him and have him backing away, he rationalises that it's not his fault that you've got 'carried away' and that he'll pass time with you.

Shopper Characteristics

Major Fast Forwarder and Future Faker – he may be the Frank Abagnale of relationships. Remember the film *Catch Me If You Can?*
Has a complicated relationship with the truth – he's often surprised that certain things aren't challenged and then sort of gets 'carried away' and

adds on more lies.

Tunnel vision about the way he conducts his life – it's not that he's unaware that he could be different in relationships; he just chooses not to and based on his fears doesn't see another way.

Likely to be a heavy computer, internet and text user.

May live far away or be based in the same area code, but has strange reasons for why you don't see him.

Secretly attached, engaged, married, separated or still getting over an ex – he'll have great justifications for why he is doing this.

In a position of authority or power – the amount of women in fantasy relationships with army guys and cops is quite scary.

May have a history of gaining cash, material goods, career moves etc from women.

Floater – either hangs around on the fringes socially or bounces around from group to group. Don't be surprised if his friends don't really know very much about his private life.

Can be very routine keeping contact or interactions in 'time slots' and reluctant to adjust his schedule in any way.

Heavy collector of attention – his interactions give him a boost of confidence and convince him that he's being and doing more than he is.

Masking low confidence so collects attention but then cuts it off before anyone gets too close.

Or has distinctly narcissistic tendencies so it's like he treats the world like one big harem to stroke his ego.

Do not be surprised if he has fabricated qualifications or jobs.

Gets sexual on and offline very quickly even if it doesn't get consummated.

Perfectionist with his own dreamy ideals that he may fantasise with you about.

Introverted and playing it safe.

Sends texts with no name on them or quite vague and general – doesn't want to mix your name up with anyone else's.

History of cheating or dates several people at a time.

May have no relationship history due to lots of short-term experiences although that's not to say he won't fill in the gaps on his 'relationship CV' with lies and exaggerations.

Relationships all end around the same time and may even claim the same reasons for each demise.

May use porn excessively or be into hardcore stuff.

Possibly has a secret life of dabbling in prostitutes, escorts, dominatrixes, dogging in car parks, swinging, three- and foursomes and sleeping with both sexes. Either that or he's roped you into it.

Sometimes he's juggling so many dalliances, he could do with setting up a call centre…

Like you, he thinks the 'right' person would prompt him to change his ways.

Jaded, cynical and even angry about dating, relationships, and women, which may stem from his childhood or from difficult experiences.

In fact, may be greatly affected by the breakup of his own parents relationship, abandonment, or loss through death, making him fear having anything beyond transient, fleeting, or distant interactions.

Veers between believing his own hype too much and being flattered by other people's aspirations and then panicking about being and doing these things in reality or on a consistent basis.

If he's ever managed a relationship of any length, it's likely that he's at the very least had inappropriate interactions with others or has had an emotional affair.

Facebook is like attention porn – a giant playground where he can present a front and track down exes and brief dalliances and get off on even the most minor of attention and conversations.

Prescriber – one day you're happy and having a laugh (or so you think) and the next day it's "I don't think that this is working."

May have been accused of stalking, had a 'misunderstanding' that has triggered a restraining order or arrest, and may have scant regard for privacy.

THE SHOPPERS

The Dreamer

Floating through life with his moving goalposts and his vision of perfection that he doesn't communicate, he's like all Fallback Girls – in search of a feeling. He knows, even if he won't admit it, that he's not likely to experience this feeling, which means he can dream away to his hearts content, absolving himself from responsibility because it's not his fault that he hasn't met the 'right' woman or been in the 'right' circumstances. He'll talk about things that he'd like to do and you'll get the impression that because he's sharing his dreams with you and even implying that you're part of them, that you must have a future. Two Dreamers together is messy and initially he may be excited by your fantasy and want to partake until it seems that you expect, need, and want too much and are encroaching on his own lack of realism. He'll tell you that you need to 'get real' while being a fully paid up member of LaLa Land himself. When he's not with another Dreamer, he can appear very distant while often being exacting and demanding. He'll blame you for why it's not working and it's not unusual to find him impossible to live with.

Online Tramp

Often spreading himself thin, he loves Fast Forwarding and Future Faking online. If collecting attention is his primary motivation, he'll be winking, messaging, and possibly sending dick shots to several women at a time – I kid you not. If high speed romance is his thing, he'll approach you, send a few emails, speed up to flirty and possibly even sexual comments, say he can't wait to meet up, ask for your number or more pictures and then disappear all in the space of 24 hours or within a few days. If he thinks he's Don Juan, he'll seduce you with words over several weeks or even months.

It may start out fairly calm, but the intensity will build and he may sound perfect aka too good to be true. He might have a sob story on repeat – I refer to this as This One Time at Band Camp in *Mr Unavailable and the Fallback Girl* - and talk about meeting up, going away together, or even moving in. Whatever his motives, even though he may deny it, he's been pressing the Reset Button and likely has a trail of virtual romances. Don't be surprised if he's attached or 'seeing' several women. He may consider himself 'shy' and 'sensitive', often being more confident online and assuming a persona that's an exaggeration, or even an outright fabrication. Of course, he'll still control the pace of contact and will suddenly start having unexplained (or poorly explained) periods of being incommunicado where you end up chasing him or sitting at home panicking.

Shy Guy

Catching out women everywhere, he's the man that many women fill in the blanks with and see meaning where there is no meaning. He's often asked out because he doesn't make a move, but appears to have some level of interest, possibly because he's hanging around. By getting you to do the legwork, he lets himself off the hook and, combined with your overactive imagination, it means that this can all become a rather tiresome game of smoke and mirrors, but not much else. Don't be surprised if he pulls the master stroke of saying that he only accepted the date because you asked or that you've imagined the whole thing, that you are 'just friends', or that he slept with you a few times because he didn't have the heart to say no. Also don't be surprised if he's 'getting over his ex' or involved with someone else.

Text Tramp

The best way to illustrate this is with a true story. A reader told me that for several months, a guy from her office texted her numerous times each day, often while sitting several seats away from her on the subway or in the office. The texts were flirty, suggestive, some ambiguous and definitely more than a work colleague. She asked him out and he knocked her back claiming that he doesn't date people from work. He also implied she had read more into things than existed. The TT is a major attention collector, often sending out one ambiguous text to several women to see who bites. He often doesn't act upon any of his text dalliances or may even have some poor woman somewhere that thinks she's his girlfriend. He is managing a Narcissistic Harem by text and kids himself that he's someone special because he has 'all' these women texting. He let's himself off the hook by telling himself that surely no one would think it's a relationship or that he's that interested if all he's doing is sending texts. Beware!

Multiple Daters

Possibly merging his role with The Phantom, the vanishing act guy from *Mr Unavailable and the Fallback Girl*, he's a permanent dater, unwilling to pin himself down to one woman although he may Future Fake that it's a possibility. As The Dreamer with your inclination to go off on a relationship tangent, you may have rationalised that you're the 'most special' or that he's off doing some really important stuff why he can't be with you all of the time. While some Multiple Daters are upfront about what they do and even get off on you all breaking your back to be chosen, many don't and it's this duplicity and the ability to make each woman feel like they're the centre of his universe when he's around them, that can be very misleading for The Dreamer and fan the illusionary flames. In search of perfection or just thinking that he's an amazing catch with too many fish in the sea to be locking himself down to one woman, he often won't correct you even when you do say things to him that imply you think you're more involved than you are, because he may find your attention and naivety flattering. Of course, if and when things get out of hand, he may disappear or even call you a 'psycho'.

Returning Childhood Sweetheart

The most likely candidates to become involved with are 'old flames' who are often still attached to someone else or are looking to reconnect with their 'youth' and have a trip down memory lane – this is something I refer to as The Returning Childhood Sweetheart in *Mr Unavailable and the Fallback Girl*. Exploiting the 'history' between you both... even if the history is flimsy or even very painful and unhealthy, you get the 'Friend Request' on Facebook or the email touching base via the alumni site and, if you're vulnerable and/or looking to escape real life, it's not long before it slips into inappropriate.

THE TRUTH ABOUT LIES

Do you know why some people are able to get their lies believed? It's because there's just enough truth, even if it's very minimal, to make the lie plausible.

As a Dreamer involved with a Shopper, no matter in how limited a capacity, you are able to lie to yourself because what little crumbs they've fed you can make the illusions plausible to you.

As a Shopper, they can lie to themselves about who they are and what they do, because you overvaluing their crumb contribution, putting it through the exaggeration oven and turning it into a loaf, along with what you say about them, all the contact, the attention, ego stroking, and even the easy sex if it goes that far, suggest that the illusions they have of themselves are plausible.

Even if you, for example, were fantasising on your own without input from the 'prop' that is Mr Unavailable, you can always rationalise that the feelings you have are real, making the fantasy plausible. After all, it's only human for us to wonder how we can have 'all of these feelings' and them 1) not be 'real' or 2) not be reciprocated.

THE LONG-SHOT MENTALITY

Only put off having a real relationship in the real world to some point in the future, if you're willing to die having never experienced it or making a damn good stab at trying, and trying, and trying again.

Your choices are being dictated by not only a desire to remain in your uncomfortable comfort zone, but also by a fear of failing at relationships, fear of risking yourself so much that it would hurt, and fear of being absolute and committing. So, instead, you cater to your beliefs and the self-fulfilling prophecy and opt into situations that really only have an outside chance of working out – yep, improbable and impossible. Fantasy relationships are based around the **long-shot mentality**.

Beliefs are premises that you hold to be true and what you believe is often unconsciously reflected in your actions. Unavailable relationships are the result of negative and unrealistic beliefs about love, relationships and yourself. If you didn't do things in line with what you believe, you'd have to change them – as you're unavailable and engaging in fantasy relationships, this is avoided at all costs for fear of being vulnerable and having to get uncomfortable and more importantly, take action. Your choices (including what you don't do) work in tandem with your beliefs, and, based on these, you predict what you think is likely to happen, which creates your **self-fulfilling prophecy**.

If you actually managed to gain love and a relationship out of these situations, it would be the equivalent of getting love against the odds.

Whatever you believe has caused you to end up being a *Dreamer* and *Fallback Girl*, it's not that what you believe is absolutely true in the wider sense, but what you believe is true in the context of your beliefs and the type of relationships you engage in.

Dreamers and, actually, Fallback Girls in general, tend to believe stuff like:

I've tried really hard to find a relationship or even the perfect mate and there's no one out there. Of course what you may neglect to mention is that you've tried to find it with your 'type' or haven't left the house, been off your laptop, or been on a date or out to social occasions in new places in a long time.

The world is full of fucked up people. This is seeing the world through distortion glasses that say that everything and everyone is unsafe, which is just not true. In truth, you're saying you don't want to do the work involved in having to learn to trust, use your judgement, and take risks. It's also like declaring yourself doomed and ultimately, it writes off the chance of trying because there's 'no point'.

Men/women/people always let me down. The plan is then to avoid disappointment by living in your unconscious where you have the illusion of never experiencing disappointment.

The only person that can make me happy is my 'type'. Yes, a type that you're either not actually having a relationship with or who you've even had previous relationships with that have proved to be unsuccessful.

The only person that can make me happy is my ex. You're declaring that happiness lies in your past, which is over, so it's like you believe that happiness is 'done'.

It's very difficult for someone to understand what I need from a relationship. Telling yourself that your needs are immensely difficult or special, actually only exacerbates the fact that you have unrealistic ideas about what your needs are, or the capability of them being met.

If someone truly loves you, they'll know what you need and expect. This is incredibly unrealistic. Love doesn't give mind-reading abilities – you actually think that when you love someone you know what they need. Funny, if you examine what you believe their needs are, it'll be what you think you need.

If they loved me, they'd do what I want and I'd always feel happy. You think love and an 'ideal relationship' is perfection. Of course this means that normal parts of loving relationships such as conflict, difficult times etc, frighten you.

If they loved me, they'd change. This is tied to a fundamental belief about your feelings having the power to change the behaviours, values, character etc of another person. You're giving yourself superhuman powers – yep, fantasy. You're just not that powerful.

What you must immediately understand about a fantasy relationship, is that you cannot experience failure at something that either doesn't exist or you've already subconsciously or even consciously accepted failure at. The fantasy relationship is a long shot, so it means that whatever professed desires and needs you make, they're faux goals. On some level you knowing that it's not going to work out and that there are in fact a lot of illusions, is actually liberating you from the responsibility that comes with putting both feet in and being emotionally available with someone else who is doing the same.

It's a faux goal, and when in retrospect it feels like you've created an incredible amount of pain for yourself, it's an own goal as well.

The long shot mentality has this fantasy reward that if it does come through, then you imagine basking in the glow of being made the exception to the rule and having your three-legged horse, or even busted-up donkey, run and win like a four-legged thoroughbred. But it's a fantasy and you'll notice in fantasies that you imagine all the glory without the problems or the responsibility...

If you've been involved in relationships where there's too much fantasy, not enough human interaction, or they're unavailable in other ways, or even married/attached, you are slipping your problematic fear of failure, making mistakes and commitment behind their somewhat more 'obvious' issues and/or a fantasy cloud.

SO, WHO'S THE MYSTERY PERSON IN YOUR FANTASIES?

Whether you're involved with a Mr Unavailable who is acting like a prop for you to put all of your feelings on, or to move around your vision of an ideal relationship, or you've retreated to a fantasy vision, it may surprise you to discover that who you fantasise about is a Mr Unavailable.

Your ideal partner in an 'ideal relationship' *is* Mr Unavailable.

Aside from the fact that you're either projecting your illusions onto a very real Mr Unavailable in your life, or you've actually made a man up or latched onto an image of an ex that's out of the picture/a celebrity/dead person etc, how you see things and what you're fantasising about is a clash of beliefs and expectations.

Who you envision in your fantasies isn't a real representation.

You've either exaggerated a real person that does exist by putting them on a pedestal and pumping them up, or you have taken aspects of a very real unavailable person as a basis of your fantasy, and then tagged onto it that they will love you unconditionally, make you feel all of the things that you don't feel for yourself and that others in real life have failed to inspire, and that they'll think, act, and speak as you'd want them to, plus added all of your ideas of what relationships are about, and then conjured up your ideal relationship and person.

When I looked back over my relationships and emotional habits, I recognised that I'd taken my painful experiences with my father, drawn a halo around it and created an image of the father I 'would' and 'should' have had in an ideal world. This wasn't a conscious thing and when you throw in the fact that I didn't know anything about values, boundaries and healthy relationships, and, in fact, had grown up with some rather unhealthy examples, I had very unrealistic and, in fact, idealistic expectations and ideas about relationships and the person who would love and 'make me' happy.

I took my Mr Unavailable father plus my expectation of being loved unconditionally (the unhealthy version – loving without limits, boundaries and self-love), plus my expectations of a healthy relationship and then equated this as my ideal man. This actually equated to Mr Unavailable, which in turn equates to expecting all of these things from an unlikely source.

Every time a Fallback Girl becomes involved and remains with a Mr Unavailable, then complains about his behaviour and wishes he was different, it's like being attracted to unavailable qualities and then complaining that he doesn't behave like an available healthy partner and fantasising that he was different, while at the same time not being attracted to different, available men because they're available.

Unavailable relationships and within them, fantasy relationships are reflections of a particular person that's at the root of the inspiration (often a parent/carer, ex, or even an abuser), with selective ideas and characteristics that you've added on with your expectations that have no basis and are actually incompatible, conflicting, and sometimes even convoluted. They fuel relationships, fantasy and real, that are set to fail which inadvertently and often quite consciously, creates a self-fulfilling prophecy.

Fantasising lets you off the hook because you can convince yourself that who you aspire to be with doesn't exist but that it's the only thing that's right for you (you assume you imagine 'correctly'), so you have 'no choice' but to rely on your imagination.

From the moment you start thinking about the fact that you don't truly believe that relationships like the one you want exist, or that the person who feels, acts and thinks a certain way doesn't exist, or that love isn't 'out there' for you, or that it's unsafe, or that you need to make an exception to your normal standards for someone, or are, in fact, hoping, wishing, praying and even wheedling them into changing so that they can make you the exception to their rule, you're actually admitting that how you see things, what you want and expect and, more importantly, what you believe is a fantasy. This makes you unavailable for an available relationship while hankering for a literally unavailable man.

UNDERSTANDING THE

UNAVAILABLE DANCE

As a Fallback Girl, you've mastered the art out of making a lot out of a little. While at Tesco (a British supermarket), 'Every little helps', this doesn't extend to emotionally, physically and spiritually unavailable men who have convinced themselves that what they give is greater than it is in actuality. This is fundamentally why Mr Unavailables get so much play – women all over the world keep pumping them up, seeing more potential than exists, and allowing them to get away with extracting as much benefit as they can without having to commit or at times, even be halfway decent.

While he may not consciously appear to take note of you not being as realistic about him and the relationship as you should be, he subconsciously registers that he is 'safe' from having to make good on any promises or false 'specifications' that he's provided about himself and the relationship, plus he also knows that he's safe from having to do the things that he fears – risk, be intimate and truly commit. When he registers your lack of realism, he also recognises that he is free of the burden of 1) really having to try, or 2) being responsible. After all, by you opting out of the present, he can't technically be responsible for failing to measure up to your own expectations and vision. Like you, this also liberates him from failing at something that he'd always known on some level that he expected it to fail, but it also gives him the freedom to have things on his terms.

You slot in well with his behaviour because for everything that he does, you're doing something that caters to the dynamic and that essentially allows the 'dance' to continue. I explain these core behaviours in *Mr Unavailable and the Fallback Girl*, but it's important to look at these in the context of a fantasy relationship.

HE BLOWS HOT AND COLD AND YOU BECOME THE PURSUER

By fluctuating the temperature of the relationship and his actions, Mr Unavailable essentially confuses the crap out of you while achieving his aim of managing down your expectations and ensuring that you don't get too close. The fact that this can continue over a period of time happens because all of this blowing hot and cold caters to some of your worst fears where you wonder if the change is down to something you've said or done, or because you're 'not good enough', providing the trigger for you to go hot in pursuit.

You pursue in an attempt to stem what you perceive as feelings of rejection and abandonment, while at the same time feeling like you're more attracted to him now that you know that it's definitely a long shot.

This then becomes a classic Bait and Switch, because all of a sudden it's gone from possible signals from him to you having to step up your effort to get even a fraction of the original attention. As the Shopper, who spreads himself thin and is always looking around, you making yourself available in spite of the fact that he's showing his true colours, lets him know that you're an option. This means that if you were just chatting online, he might think you're good for touching base for an ego stroke. Or if you slept together once, he recognises you'll be handy for a booty call. Or if you seem so interested and adoring in spite of very little happening between you both, he'll feel free to drop by periodically, whether it's virtual or face to face, when he's in need of an ego stroke.

As a Dreamer, you want the fantasy (the hot behaviour) to come back, no matter how brief that hot behaviour actually existed for. You've attached yourself to the idea and potential so you don't want the fantasy to end and have to deal with real life. That and even if it was brief, you don't want to deal with what feels like a rejection. You then become like a debt collector hunting down what you believe you're owed instead of accepting that reality has arrived and it doesn't look too good.

His actions serve as a rather rude interruption to your romantic reverie. While holding onto the fantasy in spite of his actions, you spend an incredible amount of time living in the past, because you're rehashing memories of when he desired you – they feel good. Sometimes, the stark reality is that you may be taking what amounts to a very brief period of time (days or hours even), and seeing far too much meaning where there is no meaning. When he blows cold and lukewarm, you cloak yourself in the feelings from the hot phase and, when that's not enough, you deny, rationalise and minimise so that you can convince yourself that the hot is coming soon. Unfortunately, from the moment that how you talk and think about someone is based in the past, especially off the back of what can often be a short period of time (days, weeks, or months), it means that the relationship is over…you just haven't accepted it.

Recognising your fantasy ways, he discovers that he's able to use the **Reset Button**, which is where he gives himself liberal licence to reset the relationship to whatever point that he feels most comfortable with, which effectively amounts to erasing the past.

This in turn works for you as the Dreamer, because you seem to have a selective case of **Relationship Amnesia** that lets you hold onto the fantasy. This is where you seem to suffer partial or total memory loss about events, feelings and experiences relating to the true nature of your relationship. Typically, it's when they say or do something positive and unprompted that promptly drowns out all the negative stuff, or when you mentally latch on to even the smallest of what you view as positives.

I've heard from women who have been 'involved' with men who have literally dropped by a couple of times a year for several years. They have genuinely believed that they had something very meaningful going on and when they've discovered that he invariably chases tail for the other 363/364 days of the year or is in fact attached, they've felt territorial, 'hoodwinked' and, in some of the worst cases, convinced themselves that the situation has arisen out of him needing to sort his life out elsewhere.

You are too heavily invested in the idea of the relationship with little interest and investment in the reality of it and, as a result, who he is hasn't been reconciled with reality. Even if you took the top line information of him blowing hot and cold without digging beyond it, the reality of his flip flapping ways should be communicating to you that he's inconsistent and even disrespectful, which means that you cannot 'rely' on a stable vision of a relationship with him. Sticking with the fantasy helps you to avoiding 'full' 'rejection' and 'abandonment', so you end up being blinded by your feelings, and hot in pursuit of what really amounts to hot air.

HE KEEPS THINGS ON HIS TERMS... YOU MAINTAIN THE DRAMA METER

Mr Unavailable is a 'driver' which means that, even if you manage to shift things to 'your terms' or what you perceive to be a mutual place, he will gradually or even sometimes very aggressively, take things back to his comfort zone – the Status Quo. On a scale of 1-10, he likes his relationships at 5. Of course with your fantasy ways, you probably want it at a nine, a ten, or even a twenty... He uses blowing hot and cold to yank you up and down the scale and this actually caters to your drama-seeking ways because, the truth is, you're not comfortable when it feels like things are going good and, even though you will complain and engage in plenty of negative self-talk, you actually feel more comfortable when the relationship is at the lower end of the scale. Of course you may find it difficult to admit this, but here's the thing:

As a Dreamer, you're all about the long shot – you have a fantasy of things and have on some level accepted failure at it, so when you're at the beginning of a relationship and it's in the 'hot phase', while you may feel excited, joyous, desired, aroused, loved, needed, cared for etc, it's not long before anxiety starts to creep in. Aside from expecting the other shoe to drop, you're actually afraid of being responsible and accountable in the real world, experiencing conflicts that invariably come along, being vulnerable and, of course, having to commit.

You become concerned that if this is all real, you'll have to stretch yourself in the real world.

As a result, it's not uncommon for you to sabotage and essentially 'get in there first'. You might pick a fight, withdraw contact, pour out all your feelings and expectations in a torrent, suspecting that with him being Mr Unavailable that he'll back off, or try to speed things up and make it 'real', knowing that this will send alarm bells because it will interrupt his own fantasy. You might start to feel like you're 'choking' with the possibilities of what might happen, so you will say and do whatever is necessary to lessen the anxiety as well as the sense of having to be vulnerable, realise reality, or even having to be responsible. You can then always tell yourself that even if you did do something to provoke the ending that it was only inevitable because you had suspected it anyway and were sparing yourself further heartache. Then when things calm down, the fantasy returns in full force and you pursue it again.

While for many Fallback Girls, trying to get a 10 relationship from

65

a stuck at 5 man is their competitive spirit, as a Dreamer, sticking with a reluctant or outright disinterested man and pursuing your fantasy does cater to your need to seek love against the odds, which is the long-shot mentality, but you're at the same time catering to your drama-seeking ways and, of course, the self-fulfilling prophecy. While you still prefer fantasy to reality, creating and living in drama helps to stop you making a relationship a reality.

HIS ACTIONS DON'T MATCH HIS WORDS... AND NEITHER DO YOURS

In effect, being in unavailable relationships, and persisting in them as a matter of habit, is actually making a commitment to being uncommitted. This means that any talk that you're doing about being committed is really a fantasy if you keep going back to an empty Mr Unavailable well, putting your bucket down there, and attempting to get commitment water.

As a Dreamer, you take this to a new and interesting level, because you have a far greater degree of inaction in your life, due to the fact that not only do you spend an excessive amount of time in your unconscious, but at times you're not even participating to even be having this commitment chit-chat in the first place.

Mr Unavailable's words don't match because he does things that are out of sync with his true mentality – he's unavailable for the type of relationship that you claim to want and that he even claims to want, and has the reluctant mindset to match, yet there he is dating, shagging it up, talking about the future and even marriage and babies, chasing you back up when you finish it with him, and generally appearing to be in the market for commitment.

Whether it's intentional or not, Mr Unavailable is a **Future Faker**, using a mixture of misleading actions and words to give the impression of a future, making it easier to get what he wants in the present. As the future starts to catch up, he has to put an end to the 'big dream' that he's sold you, by behaving like a jackass and/or disappearing. If you allow him to press the Reset Button at a later date, he gets a clear message that you don't really need the future to happen, you just need it to be talked about and dangled.

Some Mr Unavailables would happily argue that they truly meant it when they gave you that impression of a future. I'm sure many of these men actually believe this, but that's a fantasy as well, because you will discover if you do a bit of digging that they have form for this behaviour – you are not the first woman that has been spun this future and then had the rug ripped from under you by him. It's also a carelessness – someone who has genuine intentions to be around and knows that with integrity comes the responsibility of matching your actions with your words, doesn't say things that they're not going to follow through on. It's all very well chalking it up to good intentions and then going, 'Oops, I did it again! I thought I'd have a go at dating or having a relationship but have changed my mind,' but the truth is, that just like the person who blags their way into a job and doesn't actually have the skills, he doesn't have the actions and mindset of someone who is actually in the market for a committed relationship.

If he was in the market for a genuine, mutually fulfilling relationship, he'd know that you cannot talk and fantasise your way to instant intimacy and an instant relationship. Real relationships grow and take action.

Equally, Fallback Girls have always been able to kid themselves, that because they're fighting so hard to 'win' Mr Unavailable, and are talking and thinking a lot, as well as taking them back numerous times, trying to change themselves or him, and basically sinking their efforts into poor investments, that it means that they're the chief worker and contributor in their relationships and that they obviously want commitment. Now while I'm not suggesting that a great deal of effort isn't being put in, it's a limited effort in a limited man who yields limited relationships because he is limited emotionally and limited in his capacity to commit.

When you really want a relationship and a healthy, committed, mutual one at that, you don't seek it from unavailable men and you in fact, tell them to shag off when they're not prepared to step up. You can tell a hell of a lot about your true actions, motivations, and how much you want to commit by the relationships you engage in – your actions do not match those of someone who takes action, never mind wants commitment. You also wouldn't be so easily sold.

As a Dreamer, a Future Faking Mr Unavailable is like having someone on board to validate some of your wildest dreams. It's like: 'Wow! Someone else dreams like I do? Hot diggity damn!' Unfortunately, you don't recognise that there's something wrong when you hardly know someone and they're talking about a future that isn't reflective of the amount of time you've known one another, their current actions, or even just a moderate level of normality. You may argue, 'Oh, but what's normal? Normal is what you make it,' but, really, only people who are unrealistic don't maintain boundaries and try to be the exception to the rule on some pretty shady stuff say this kind of thing.

Is it really 'normal' to meet someone on a dating site at 1pm, to have exchanged twenty emails and texts by 9pm, for them to be sending you a penis shot by 11pm, and for you to be thinking, 'This could be it.'?

And this is where, as a Dreamer, you have to recognise that you are sometimes, or even often, Future Faking yourself. Of course this actually 'works' for you, in that, on some level, you don't believe his Future Faking, especially as you'll already be starting to feel some private anxiety about where this is all headed. The fact that he's being 'dreamy', while it on one hand feels attractive and 'perfect' for you, on the other hand, it actually acts as a warning signal that confirms your self-fulfilling prophecy – you know this is not going to work out because you know that you are dreamy, you're chasing the long-shot, and you don't match your words with actions and are, in fact, not expecting this to become reality.

When a lot of your effort is mental and 'virtual' with you veering between living in the past or focusing on potential, you are a Dreamer that is bullshitting herself about how active she is really being. If you began matching your actions and words, not only would you find yourself based in reality, but the Mr Unavailables of this world would no longer be attractive to you.

HE LIKES FAST FORWARDING... YOU DINE OFF ILLUSIONS

It's very easy to be whisked off into a fantasy and miss some very obvious signs that all is not well, when you are moving at such a speed – emotionally and physically – that reality either flashes by so that you don't notice the details, or you're blinded to it, near dazzled by the dream.

Fast Forwarding is in itself a form of Future Faking and it refers to when someone sweeps you up in a tide of intensity while pursuing and/or in the relationship that you end up missing crucial information about them. While they will Future Fake, they'll also behave intensely by putting so many demands on you (emotional, sexual, wanting to be with you all the time), that you believe that the level of intensity you're experiencing is what is on offer and also reflective of the intensity of their feelings for you. You'll then use a

number of the things that they fast forward you with as
basis to trust them.

When one or both of you are doing stuff like pushing for emotional and sexual commitment very quickly, claiming or thinking, 'This is it!' or 'You're the one!' even though you've only known one another a wet minute, having a sense of ownership very quickly, pursuing intensely, introducing one another to people, it all creates this fantasy that you're both so fabulous and your love is so grand that you guys don't need to do the things that 'others' do, like taking a bit of time to get to know one another, looking for genuine signs and action that build your levels of trust in them and also your confidence in feeling safe in disclosing your feelings, and sleeping together, and not needing to feed each other a fairy tale to keep interested.

As you're very illusion led, your head is already in the clouds when you meet Mr Unavailable, so when he does what he does anyway, you won't see the wood for the trees.

Fast Forwarding is perfect for the Shopper who may literally speed his way through his faux intimacy cycle in hours (brief liaisons on dating sites or one-night stands), days (more liaisons on dating sites and quick flings), weeks (whirlwind romances), or a few months (long-distance romances, living the dream relationship for a few months). Whatever he's up to, it will come to an end.

You're not engaging in behaviours to be the person you fantasise being, nor are you even realistic about what the actions are that would lead to being that person, plus you set yourself such a long shot for a relationship that you don't really ever have to try. Mr Unavailable recognises that you're an ideal partner when his actions don't match his words and you're right there at his side not matching your own – he knows he's in good company. Shoppers recognise when you're willing to partake in texting all the time, moving at high speed at the beginning, believing in their hype, and waxing lyrical about things that neither of you are making a reality, that you're OK to dream with.

It's bad enough to get caught up with your average Mr Unavailable, but as a Dreamer with a Shopper, it's like the Inception of relationships – a dream, within a dream, within another dream.

You can both be your fantasy selves – he gets to project his vision of you on you, and vice versa plus he gets to put forward a false or exaggerated self, as do you. It becomes difficult to discern fact from fiction and, in the end, because you're both too idealistic, each of you taking any real action negates the basis for a relationship with one another, because it shrinks the odds by creating genuine needs, expectations and desires and, along with them, the responsibility and commitment that comes with the package, which means that the relationship is no longer attractive.

HE LOVES CASUAL RELATIONSHIPS… YOU CONFUSE SEX WITH LOVE AND A CONNECTION

Never before has it been so easy to live in a fantasy, simply because the style of relationship that allows for it is far more commonplace and the means of keeping in touch, or even having a vague sense of connection, have been made easier thanks to technology. In 'olden times' if you were having a fantasy relationship, it was somewhat more difficult with a backdrop of the societal expectation being some form of out in the open commitment. It would have been obvious to you and others that a relationship wasn't happening or going anywhere, or that you were, in fact, alone.

Now, the world is full of people who maintain pseudo connections, friendships and 'relationships' through distant communication – text messages, email, instant messenger, Facebook, Twitter, dating sites and the list goes on. There are people who appear to have hundreds, if not thousands, of 'friends', who not only have an amplified persona online, but who in real life actually have very few actual friends. We're increasingly relaxed about dating and relationships, with all sorts of terms for basically shagging and 'hanging out' without labels, such as Friends With Benefits, Fuck Buddies, 'casual dating' (I know, we're even trying to water that down), hook-ups and booty calls, and this in turn has relieved a lot of the pressure to take action and essentially opened the floodgates to thinking whatever you want to think without clarification or regard for the reality of the impact of these situations.

This is the perfect fertile ground for Mr Unavailable, who has managed the art of getting more for less, often while operating with some serious double standards where he gets to have his cake and eat it while often penalising you for participating in the marginalised arrangement that he's pushing in the first place. The Shopper doesn't like to 'label' things or, even if he does put a name to your involvement, he backtracks on this by undermining it and behaving in ways that affect the progression, consistency, balance, commitment and intimacy of the relationship. Even though there can appear to be hallmarks of a relationship, it essentially ends up being casual.

With your assuming ways, you keep believing that because there is 'friendship noise' and sex, that ipso facto a relationship could and should follow, even though, at the same time, you get distinct signs, even if you choose to ignore them, that actions and words don't match.

Sex is the low hanging fruit for many Fallback Girls because it's perceived as being 'easier' than actual emotional intimacy. At the same time, sex is often mistaken for emotional intimacy, so in a 'casual' arrangement, even one that's incredibly ambiguous and barely even there, it can cause the nature of the relationship and your respective feelings to be greatly exaggerated. Mistaking a sexual connection for a love connection is a fantasy anyway – you're assuming that someone who you experience this with, whether it's physically or virtually, frequently or infrequently, in a relationship or out of one, is someone in possession of other characteristics, qualities and values that you desire and that they can make you happy and give you the relationship you want.

For Dreamers, just talking with someone, trusting a little, can feel like a huge effort, so when you start sharing explicit texts/emails/calls or sleeping together, when he starts acting up afterwards, instead of admitting that he's not who you thought he was and registering reality, you hold onto the fantasy because you want to validate your reasons to do these things with him in the first place rather than admit your mistake. This is the Justifying Zone, a special place where all Fallback Girls end up. From this point onwards, you're being very unrealistic about him and overestimating the connection.

In order to experience that love connection, you do need to be emotionally intimate and sex is not even close to being an adequate substitute. There's no way that you can be experiencing the connection that you think you are if you avoid your feelings and vulnerability.

Sex within a loving relationship is part of a love connection, but sex outside of this is just sex and to persist in thinking otherwise, is to delude yourself and open yourself up to, at best, being taken advantage of and, at worst, being abused. You're placing too great an emphasis on the power of sex and, again, you're trying to skip over all of the vital things that you would expect to exist between two people experiencing a love connection because, in your fantasy world, you don't need to.

All of this focus on the sex and the 'moments' around it then has you living in a bubble. You're chasing a feeling, and it's actually a fantasy feeling and each attempt at being with him and pushing for things to go somewhere, is like an attempt to recapture that feeling. Even when you stop interacting with him, in spite of very good reasons not to continue, you hold onto your vision and cling to the feeling, mourning what you thought you lost or think you're owed. All from sex or sexual attraction. If you make the mistake of going back, he continues to get the casual relationship, giving him all of the fringe benefits of a relationship without commitment or reality. In turn, you keep thinking that the fantasy is a possibility because he's not full on knocking you back, and so it's lather, rinse, repeat.

HE DEALS IN CRUMB RATIONS OF COMMITMENT... YOU'VE BECOME A DISGRUNTLED CUSTOMER

The perfect illustration of Mr Unavailable's fantasy ways, is his tendency to put his commitment crumbs through a magical exaggeration oven, and then shazam, they're suddenly loaves. In reality, if he were around someone who has themselves firmly planted in reality and has a realistic view of what constitutes a mutual partnering and effort, as in consistent, concerted, intimate, balanced, progressive, committed effort, his crumbs would look like crumbs.

To you, with your illusionary ways, his crumbs act as 'props' that provide inspiration for your own fantasy vision.

The habitual Mr Unavailable over the course of his relationship history has mastered the art of making a lot out of a little and has had much help along the way from Fallback Girls who have been more than willing to blow smoke up his bum while he's standing on a pedestal. He just doesn't view his relationship capabilities in reality and so may actually believe that he's operating at full throttle, when it could be as little as 10% of the effort of someone who is putting both of their feet in. By not committing to an outcome, whether it's to put both feet into a relationship or to remove himself completely, he's also liberated from being truly accountable and responsible, while at the same time often managing to still enjoy the fringe benefits of a relationship from you.

The key with the Shopper is that not only will he fail to stump up commitment when it's crunch time, but when you finally step outside of the situation and attempt to view it with a modicum of objectivity and reality, it suddenly seems so ridiculous that this person can keep spinning the fantasy, often in retrospect in what are ridiculous periods of time. It will appear bonkers that he was talking about meeting your parents or taking you to a wedding, when you didn't even know where he lived yet, or that he has a wife and kids that don't know of your existence.

On the scale of crumbanality (yes, I made up that word), the Shopper is often off the charts, because his crumbs are often illusions in themselves.

When it becomes apparent that he's not playing ball with the fantasy, even if it was for a matter of hours, you end up being like a disgruntled customer demanding that you get the product that you thought you were getting. You want more than he can deliver and this is the fantasy, because in this magical world where you could 'make' him 'change back' to the person you thought he was or have him follow through on what you thought would happen, he'd be making you the exception to the rule – yep, the long shot.

You trying to make him roll up those illusionary crumbs and turn them into a real loaf becomes a consuming task that frustrates you and caters to your self-fulfilling prophecy. To avoid the sense of loss and rejection, you keep trying to relive the past or make him rise to the potential that you've foreseen. You're looking for a magical ending to a situation that's far from magical or even healthy and, ultimately, instead of opting out of a poor investment, you're being stubborn and taking a major gamble that will ultimately backfire.

HE KEEPS A FOOTHOLD IN YOUR LIFE… YOU KEEP LEAVING THE DOOR AJAR

While there's no denying that Mr Unavailable is a pain in the arse who will sniff around and wedge his foot under the proverbial door so that he can keep things on his terms even when he's out of a relationship or never even had one with you in the first place, he's given free reign to do so because you keep leaving the door ajar out of a desire to live the fantasy. Him slinking around, even if it's on the peripheries of your life, actually helps you to avoid yourself, contributing to your tendency to spend too much time in your unconscious relaxing in your comfort zone.

The Shopper is a rather pesky sort – he can be pretty persistent, sending texts, emails and even voicemails even when you're blanking him (or pretending to). Time and again I've heard from women who literally have Mr Unavailables fishing around for attention like clockwork, every X amount of days, weeks or months. It's like an internal alarm goes off and they have to do a roll call and ensure that all their back-up plans and ego strokers are still on standby. However, what's more likely to be happening if you're a Dreamer is that, even if you don't reply today or tomorrow, you will feel compelled to respond to him in some capacity because the possibility that he may have spontaneously combusted into a commitment-willing available man will literally burn a hole in your fantasy back pocket.

You have no endings and no finality, so it's like being in your own never-ending story where you're seeking validation while, at the same time, as a result of these involvements, validating the negative things you believe about yourself. All of this malarkey leaves you in limbo.

The best way to ensure that you avoid making a mistake and 'failing', is to, along with having the long-shot mentality, keep the door ajar so that no matter how brief a dalliance may have been, the option is always there for the fantasy to happen. This is literally how you can have the same guy pulling the same con on you numerous times – even if you initially show some reticence, you just can't help but believe that this time, the fantasy is going to happen and you're going to ride off together into the sunset on a white horse.

You're afraid, like all Fallback Girls, that there's an off chance that he may become a better man in a better relationship with someone else.

When you consider how flimsy some of a Shopper's relationships are, it can actually seem quite ridiculous that they can feel compelled to even dip back in on someone they had a one-night stand with or only spoke to online for a couple of hours. A friend of mine has had guys she corresponded with for short periods of time on dating sites get in touch up to five years later. She blanks them, but I've actually heard from some women who were so hopeful that they threw caution to the wind and started chatting again, maybe even slept with them, only for them to bail again.

That said, you can see the extent of the 'dreaming' in this situation, when you have such a fear of 'making a mistake', that you won't even chalk up a date, email, one-night stand, or fling to a bit of fun or 'incompatibility'.

This is one of the pitfalls of dealing with Shoppers et al in brief capacities – it's easy to rationalise that as it was only a few emails/calls/texts, or a one-night stand, or a few dates that it's too harsh to judge them and write them off on this basis. After all, maybe they were going through a hard time, were busy, had a cat stuck up a tree, in a coma or whatever. I can see where you're headed with this logic, but you have to wonder:

Of all the girls, in all the world, why, when you had stopped being in touch, have they decided to get back in touch?

And this is where you can again see the synchronicity between you both – he fears making a mistake too. It's like he's peeing a ring around all of his involvements and keeping tabs out of fear that he's made a mistake and one of the women he pulled in a bar, shagged and then faded on, or with whom he corresponded on mail for a while, or who he texts for attention is actually going to be a better woman in a better relationship with someone else.

By leaving the door ajar, the fantasy is that in their absence, they've suddenly found compelling reasons to get back in touch and that the connection, no matter how brief, was so great, that they had to come back.

But you also have to ask: Why am I leaving the door ajar for these people? What have I actually witnessed or experienced that is so great, that it warrants making myself unavailable for an available relationship on the off chance that one of these people has an attack of regret and decides to pursue the fairy tale?

Him keeping a foothold in your life, even if it's in a minor capacity, can actually be all the prop that you need in order to fire up your imagination. Next thing you're telling yourself that it's a bad time, he's going through a lot, he's busy, shy, or so crazy about you that even though he has nothing of genuine value to offer, he just can't let you go. If you're lonely, or your self-esteem is low, these crumbs of attention can ease those feelings. Sadly though, all he often needs is confirmation that you're still interested (OK and possibly a shag or a sext) and this can be enough for him to go about his merry way and leave you high and dry again. What you must remember is that if you were having a real relationship, with a real mutual connection, he'd not only walk through that door, but he'd close it and stay with you, instead of leaving you to your own devices and imagination once he's got what he wants.

HE USES TIMING TO MANAGE YOU... YOU SEEM TO HAVE ALL THE TIME IN THE WORLD

Mr Unavailable has a rather complicated and somewhat convoluted relationship with time. He's often bleating that he doesn't have enough time, because you know he's busier than a world leader, or that it's the 'wrong' time, while implying that there might be a 'right' time that he doesn't intend on materialising, and messes about with the future, either avoiding it or faking one to get what he wants now. While all these shenanigans are going on, you're spending your time in an unavailable relationship, making you of course unavailable for an available one.

His space-time continuum is perfect for a Dreamer because it means that it's very difficult to have a sense of reality. Being focused on chasing a feeling and clinging to isolated moments, it's quite easy for the Shoppers and other Mr Unavailables of this world to be the short-term, reactive thinkers that they are. All of this messing about with time also allows them to play for time.

But let's be real – you're playing for time too, because by persisting in your fantasy ways, it's like you think you have all the time in the world. You wait around for him, which not only busts up your own boundaries, but, by not closing the door, you're prevented from fully grieving the relationship, accepting the loss of it, and/or the hopes and dreams you had for it, and moving on… in reality. As you don't want to be real, it's easy for you to allow him to disrespect your time because you don't value your own because you're not in reality to do so anyway.

When you're doing all this dreaming, you're very focused on what you think 'could' or 'should' happen and given a choice between getting into reality and being 100% responsible for yourself or giving the fantasy an indefinite 'run', you'll opt for the latter. Each time you consider letting it go, it becomes unpalatable, because when you consider how much time you've spent on the fantasy, to step into reality and admit this starts to feel incredibly painful and you'll want to escape these feelings, so you'll find something to cling to again that will buy you some more time.

You don't see the wood for the trees because in being so narrowly focused on avoiding your fears, you don't recognise how you avoid life itself, including the good and great things about it, plus you Future Fake yourself by gambling, often privately reasoning that you'll give 'this' a bit more time and definitely cut things off 'next time', because you don't want to deal with you, life, and anything uncomfortable that comes with it now.

All of the fantasising, denial, rationalising, minimising etc fuel the Relationship Amnesia you seem to suffer with - you forget anything inconvenient, block out anything traumatic, and focus entirely on the positive, even if, in context, it's actually rather small. When you do try to get real, these periods of blocking out reality make it difficult for you to work out what's real and what's fake, or where your culpability and his begin and end.

In truth, you don't have all the time in the world. In your imagination you do, but that's not even running off the same schedule as reality, which is why you can skip over all the things you'd have to deal with if you were engaging in the real world. When you do get a jolt and suddenly realise how your life has been impacted by your 'absence' and begin to feel like you've 'wasted' your life or are 'running out of time', it originates from the regret in recognising that a chunk of time has passed and what you're doing or your outlook hasn't really shifted. It may feel like you could begin to achieve the things you desire by focusing on the thoughts, but without the action you get left in limbo, but time marches on regardless.

There are Mr Unavailables out there who would waste no time doing what my friend refers to as 'eating up your good years' but, as a Dreamer, it's also time to recognise that you're dreaming away your life, whether you have one making a pest of himself or not. You have no control over what he chooses to do with his time, but your time is in your hands – grab it with both of them.

HE'S AN EGOTIST SEEKING PERFECTION... YOU'RE SEEKING A FEELING

Mr Unavailable is driven by a core motivation – remain distant (avoid true intimacy), which helps avoid being truly committed, which keeps him safe, while at the same time doing just enough to enjoy the fringe benefits. He has a 'wider' fantasy of what the person and the relationship looks, acts and feels like, where he'll be prepared to put himself in and commit –

unsurprisingly, it's the equivalent of perfection. Yep, Mr Unavailable has fantasy issues of his own, so really, both of you getting involved is like a clash of two idealistic people who just don't have enough of a connection to their respective emotional cores and reality to be realistic.

Along with his wider fantasy, he also has a narrower, short-term vision of what he thinks a person should be and do, and what a relationship without intimacy and commitment looks like – all the fun and the glory, without the effort. Of course he's unlikely to verbalise it as such, unless he actually pitches you some Friends With Benefits situation that makes it sound like you're about to have the best of both worlds, or he's extremely arrogant, but what he is imagining is a risk, fear, commitment and problem-free, happy clappy environment.

The dynamic in unavailable relationships is based around one person being the driver (usually him) and one being the passenger (yep, that would be you). Even in the most feeble of unavailable relationships, somehow Mr Unavailable manages to end up with things on his terms. Even if you start out being the driver, when he stops playing ball and you respond with a flurry of pandering to him, the bait and switch occurs and you're suddenly clamouring for nuggets of attention in a relationship that you felt like you were once in the driving seat of. This is why when you expect, need and want more than he's prepared to be wanted, needed and expected from, he'll blow lukewarm or cold to manage back down your expectations so that he can maintain the Status Quo – keeping things on his terms in a middle ground comfort zone.

At the same time, by having a combination of natural expectations, plus any unrealistic and unhealthy beliefs that you're projecting via your expectations, you effectively shoot yourself in the foot, as he'll deem you 'inappropriate' for the wider fantasy – you prove yourself to be unfit for perfect relationship purpose by being a combination of human (I know! Can you believe he doesn't realise this?) and a Dreamer. Of course it's very unfair, but this is a by-product of being involved with a Mr Unavailable that flip flaps, has double standards, is often guilty of the very things that he doesn't like in others, busts boundaries, wants things all on his terms and is seeking unattainable perfection to boot.

He often has no shame in saying and doing things to meet his short-term primary objectives. Unfortunately, this gives way to Future Faking and Fast Forwarding.

Of course, as a Dreamer, someone talking the future up a storm or effectively sweeping you off your feet, is music to your ears – it feels like you're going to be able to grasp that 'feeling' you're seeking.

When you have your own agenda, he can actually be pissy with you and imply, or even outright state, that you would have been together, that he would have even been 'perfect' or at least everything that he's not being, and that all of the wonderful imaginings would have happened, if it weren't for the fact that you didn't 'measure up', weren't patient enough, or didn't have a circumstance that he'd always known about from day one but has suddenly become a no-no. This can feel like a serious smack in the face, especially if you've had an intense flurry of communication or romancing.

He may have exacting standards, which will leave you feeling like you're failing and falling short. This will only serve to increase the confusion and the fantasy and illusions will be fuelled further because you will continue justifying your involvement or your feelings for him, even when they're clearly not being reciprocated and he may even be behaving like a jackass. All of the excuses, assumptions, denial, rationalising and minimising takes you further down the rabbit hole.

His dissatisfaction will be hurtful and will tap into the rejection you love to avoid, while at the same time, because you really want the fantasy, you'll convince yourself that you've 'done' something to stop it from happening – that's a fantasy as well unfortunately, one that removes him of any responsibility for your involvement because you're too eager to be the human equivalent of kitchen roll, absorbing up the blame from all directions.

This is all music to his ears because, like a typical perfectionist, he's either all right or all wrong, but not in between. In your eagerness to recapture the feeling, you behave in ways or even say things that let him off the hook, pumping up his ego while leaving you feeling deflated. It's as if you figure that the trade off is worth it, if you get that 'feeling' back. You keep remembering the 'good times' or his 'good points', but fail to recognise that by chasing a feeling that has already passed or hasn't even happened yet, that in reality, this relationship is over. Focusing on escaping anything uncomfortable and returning to 'happier' feelings, actually blinds you to the more obvious flaws in this relationship, which propels you deeper into a fantasy.

HE BREAKS OUT THE SOB STORY AND EXCUSES... YOU INFLATE YOUR EMOTIONAL AIRBAG

While your tendency to veer between living in the past and betting on potential has much to do with why you don't spend enough time and energy in the present, listening to his excuses and sob stories or even fabricating them on his behalf, can be the bread and butter of keeping up a fantasy. He just doesn't even have to try that hard because all you need is one thing to make your feelings and whatever hopes you have about this relationship real, and the rest you can pad out with denial, rationalising, minimising, and what you feel are genuine reasons for lack of input from him, failure to deliver on his (or your) proposed fantasy, or at its worst, assholic behaviour.

While of course, you may be focusing your fantasy on someone that you have no involvement with, and making up excuses off your own back, it's always important to remember that as a Fallback Girl, even one who loves to cloak herself in fantasies, you do your damndest to make yourself available for defaulting duty. This is why I have so many emails from 'understanding' women who positioned themselves in a friend, coworker or ex's life no matter how vaguely, to be their confidante-cum-armchair psychologist or whinge receptacle, to be indispensable and act as their go-to for championing them and pumping up their ego. He may claim otherwise but, the truth is, he has become used to the praise, the presence, the flattery and the sense, even if he won't admit it, that you fancy the arse off him. You'd be surprised how many of these guys will feign innocence about your interest, yet on some level in the back of their mind, they recognise that should things not work out with their current partner or they exhaust all avenues elsewhere, you'll be there.

As the comedian Chris Rock has said, women get attention from men all the time, whereas men still treat it like a novelty. Mr Available has enough cojones about him to recognise when your interest isn't platonic or when you've got the wrong idea and will set you straight and avoid you if needed. Mr Unavailable sees an *opportunity*.

It may be that his various tales and excuses aren't directly related to a relationship you think you have with him, but to a current relationship with someone else, or to his various problems which you have made yourself a part of. It could be as simple as him claiming that he's 'overwhelmed', or saying, 'Well, at least I can always rely on you to understand', and he might actually be talking about work, but you read it to be that he means it about his relationship. At the same time, you may even recognise that they're sob stories and excuses but reason that if he were in a different relationship with you treating him in the way you believe he's not being treated elsewhere, they'd cease to exist.

Once he recognises that you're buying what he's selling, he feels free to relax into his mode and, to be fair, at the same time, on some level you recognise that there isn't really anything on offer, which leaves you free to fantasise instead of being active.

What you and even he may not realise, is that there are things that he directly and indirectly says that are designed to give you a heads up on what's really going on... if you're actually listening and watching, plus they have the double-pronged use of lessening his responsibility. Unfortunately, when you receive signals that he's unavailable and/or not who you thought he was, or he slips you an excuse, retells his One Time At Band Camp tales of woe, and even sheds great big dollopy crocodile tears with no real sentiment behind them, instead of feeling the needle being ripped from the record of your dream, you actually see even bigger reasons to dream.

If you were a more realistic person, when it becomes clear that your feelings are unreciprocated, or that he's not available for an available relationship, or that he's slipping you excuses, dropping hints and guilting you into not expecting too much of him, or even crying on you to distract you, you'd recognise that something is gravely wrong with this situation and act upon the information in real time. However you don't, because all of these things provide Bingo Moments, internal light bulbs switching on when you get confirmation that he's Mr Unavailable and that this relationship is indeed a long shot, hence you're free to remain in your comfort zone of being the Dreamer. These relationships give you a purpose of being able to dream yourself into:

Feeling more purposeful than you actually are because you're not being purposeful through action.

Having a reason, no matter how flimsy, to stick around as you can absorb yourself in his drama or the bubble of your fantasy.

Being the direct solution to problems that you had no part in creating (addictions, mental health issues, his marriage etc) and that, in fact, need very different things, including him, to resolve them. You think that you represent all that he's missing and even imagine being praised and admired by others for making a positive difference to his life.

Fixing yourself by using him as a vessel to do your fantasy fixing, healing and helping, which in turn you imagine if you're successful at doing so, you'll be automatically fixed.

Being in control. After all, not only are you placing yourself in safe but uncomfortable circumstances that allow you to maintain your position of being a Dreamer, but it means that you are limiting your experiences, giving you the impression of being in control.

You're the Fallback Girl whose perception of being compassionate is actually code for dreaming.

`Compassion is sympathetic pity and concern for the misfortunes of others. (Source: Oxford Dictionaries)`

Your idea of what compassion translates as is hearing what you perceive to be misfortune, then seeing a situation or them in what you believe is the 'best light', which is actually a fantasy. The best light is actually reality.

Your tendency to put too much of you and your dreams into situations, also means that you have some funny ideas about empathy, which is the ability to put yourself in another person's shoes so that you can recognise and understand their position. Unfortunately, because you're unrealistic, you've mistaken how you see yourself and others as empathy when, in fact, it's fantasy. You put yourself in your own shoes and put a lot of energy into what you think 'could' and 'should' happen instead of what is happening, and you put yourself into others' shoes and latch onto things that you believe indicate potential for your fantasy and fill in all the gaps. This all forms the 'air' in your emotional airbag. When you kill your urge to wrap yourself around someone's supposed problems and shortcomings, you kill your urge for fantasy, so you can strip back to who you really are and influence your own life.

HE ONLY THINKS OF HIMSELF... YOU PUT THE FOCUS ON HIM

As the 'driver', not only is Mr Unavailable doing things solely on his terms, but his thoughts are very centred around him, so he just doesn't engage in a level of consideration or empathy that would take the other party into the equation. He only looks at things from his perspective and in his little fantasy world of how people work, he seems to operate under this misguided impression that if he's happy, comfortable, not bothered or whatever about a situation that, ipso facto, anyone else involved won't be either. In fact, he's so busy thinking of himself that on the occasions where Other People's Feelings prick at his conscience, he's always able to rationalise his position.

Whatever he has to give, that's what he thinks you need, so if his capacity is for a mostly virtual liaison, feeding you on a diet of text crumbs and occasional meet-ups, in his mind, it's all he has to give, so it's what you will and should be happy with. He's not a team player whether it's in his fantasy or in real life. You can really see this in action when he's The Returning Childhood 'Sweetheart', engaging in a flurry of contact, stirring up old feelings and memories, or even rewriting history, only to screw you over.

When he reaches out to you, he has this fantasy of reconnecting which in turn reconnects him with his 'old self'. He starts something that he hasn't really put a great deal of thought into, operating off impulse and living the fantasy, while at the same time on some level recognising that he's leading you up the garden path, and also telling himself that should any issues arise off the back of his big talk, that he'll cross that bridge when he comes to it. It is astounding really that someone doesn't truly think about the impact of returning to someone's life, someone who may have already suffered more than enough or had to work very hard to get over the original breakup – only someone who is already highly invested in a fantasy could behave in this manner.

Mr Unavailable is very impulsive and reactive – act now, think and backtrack later, probably in an equally impulsive and reactive manner.
He only thinks of himself. Oh he might believe he thinks of you or others, but that's a fantasy when you take a close look at his inconsistent

actions and words.

Unfortunately, Mr Unavailable has a damn good run in life, simply because there is a steady stream of women who are only too willing to make him the focal point of their lives, and it's not too great a leap to see how someone who gets such a disproportionate amount of investment from women, might start to believe that he's more considerate and empathetic than he really is. Of course, if he were a realistic person, he'd recognise that irrespective of all of the pumping up by women, he does not behave in ways that are deserving of the investment.

To fuel your fantasies, you put all of the focus on him and actually, it's not really because the sun shines out of his arse, but more because by focusing your thoughts and efforts on him, you avoid yourself and in turn lose yourself. He and your hopes for a relationship end up becoming extensions of you because you put so much of you into them, hence when they're not going according to plan, it feels like a direct blow to you.

With your fantasy ways, like all Fallback Girls, you're operating under this notion that if you give him what you think you need, that he'll reciprocate. In your mind, you reason that if someone were making you the centre of their universe, that you'd feel loved, happy and, of course, want to commit and cough up the relationship that you want – the fantasy.

This unfortunately means that it's like you're both co-existing in two separate and distinctly different fantasies, so really you're not even relating to one another. You're actually both giving to yourselves – if you were truly giving to one another or attempting to, you'd at least be spending more of your time in reality, albeit an unhealthy one.

You'll get indications that all is not well, so to keep the fantasy going, you focus on coming up with excuses why all of the things you think should have happened haven't happened, which only digs you deeper into this unhealthy relationship. As a Dreamer, you don't know where to draw the line on excuses, especially if there is very little happening between you both. You'll want to resist letting go of the excuses because it means accepting reality in exchange for them. You look around and see the rubble of your life and recognise that in focusing on him, your job performance has slid, your kids have grown without you realising it, your health has suffered, and that you've not been engaging in your life and doing things that interest you and maintaining other relationships, so it will seem easier to try to focus on him again or to get a new fantasy, than it is to face your feelings about what you've done to yourself or deal with the after effects. You'll want to put some distance between you and real-life evidence of your self-neglect.

In the aftermath, you'll actually remain in a fantasy if you focus all of your thoughts on him, obsess about the finer details and avoid your culpability, or you instead make him out to be the messiah and peg yourself as having wrecked things with a 'perfect' man. Even if your involvement is quite brief, because you've wasted no time imagining who you think he is and what your relationship might become, when it all goes tits up, it's like recovering from a nasty hangover that seems to hang around – if you don't heed the lesson, you'll get intoxicated again to avoid the pain of the fantasy not being real, and either try and focus on him again... or find someone else.

PICTURING AND POTENTIAL –

HOW TO GET 'HOOKED' ON A

FANTASY

Much like how you use your beliefs, including those that you may not have consciously acknowledged exist, you have **hooks** – reasons, excuses and stories – that tie you to a person. They invariably become your 'blind spot' because they are either one particular thing that you overvalue to such a degree that it overrides reality and any concerns you have or should have, or they represent personality traits, values and incidences that you keep mentally and verbally returning to.

These 'hooks' are what you'll cling to as reasons to:
1) feel attracted to them.
2) justify your emotional and sexual investment.
3) put them on a pedestal.
4) make excuses for them or your own actions.
5) yo-yo back and forth when you struggle to let the relationship go... even when you should.

You can be assured that if there is the presence of 'hooks' – you'll know because you keep reiterating certain things – that you are focusing on isolated and possibly irrelevant or greatly exaggerated things, instead of seeing the person and any relationship you have with them as a whole and in reality. It's not always that the hooks are untrue, but they distort your relationship because of the magnitude of 'greatness' you believe them to be in possession of which can be akin to adulation ('He's a good man'), when he's just average Joe doing things that most people take for granted as being the basics of decent behaviour instead of treating someone like they're the messiah, or in fact he may not even be that good. At times, you're also distorting the relative importance ('They're so powerful/beautiful/popular') because, really, these things do not matter a damn to your relationship if they don't add value to an actual mutually fulfilling relationship and you don't even share common values.

PICTURING – HOW TO INFLATE POTENTIAL

Hooks simply work like this: You latch or 'hook' yourself onto something and then, based on being attracted to it or at least believing it to be indicative of something 'special', or a symbol of relationship worthiness, or even a sign that this person must be a 'good person', you correlate it to the rest of them and assume that they'll possess other qualities, characteristics and values that someone you believe is 'right' for you will possess. Due to your fantasy inclinations combined with betting on potential, you end up relating with the 'hooks' or your imagination instead of the person themselves.

You work off an assumption that if you find someone attractive, or you your fantasy cogs start whirring into action, or you sleep with them in X days instead of Y weeks (or have sex with them at all), or you can't walk away, or you have no self-control and are even willing to be walked over, that there must be good reasons for it.

You persist in believing that there must be a good reason for what you're doing (or not doing) and thinking, in spite of the fact that you're not living the good reason. Your hooks represent stubbornness – in spite of compelling, sometimes even life-threatening reasons to do so, you resist and, in fact, often outright refuse to change your attitude, course and behaviour.

How you make the leap from one or a few qualities and characteristics to suddenly believing that they and the relationship have potential is called **picturing**:

```
You take pieces of information that you hear or see
(hooks) and, after over-correlating this information
and making assumptions about them as a person, you then
adjust your picture of the potential of the
relationship and your vision equates to convincing
yourself that this person is great and/or that the
relationship is worth your effort.
```

One reader told me how she was totally not interested in a guy but then he told her this really sad story and next thing you know she was picturing herself being the woman that would love him and make him feel whole again. She literally pictured herself showing up to a family gathering and people smiling at them for being a happy, beautiful couple and admiring her for what she'd brought to his life. Their children who she hadn't even met yet and knew nothing about, would look at her like a mother and would have tears in their eyes about finally being taken care of again. They'd been on three dates.

You know you've got problems when someone you hardly know tells you a sad story or shares a difficult piece of their past and, rather than listening and empathising, you're hearing the jackpot bells ringing because you've sniffed an opportunity.

Another reader told me that she wasn't really that interested in her Returning Childhood 'Sweetheart', especially because even if he was a great lay all the way back then, he was very self-absorbed and arrogant, plus she wasn't even attracted to him anymore. However, when he talked about buying a place in a particular part of the country that she liked, his job, his status at work and within the community, plus his dropped hints about being eager not to be single for long, in spite of no actual interest, she was now imagining herself at his side as his wife and even mentally decorating the property they'd live in and feeling 'full' from being married again.

It's very easy to avoid real, present day problems when you're tuned out to a fantasy frequency.

Here's a very common example – just insert common interests that you've valued:

You discover that you have a shared love of drinking fine wine, listening to obscure music from the somewhere-or-other mountains and outdoor pursuits. They're really attractive, too. You assume that with the shared interests and physical attraction, you have a lot in common and picture yourself doing all this stuff together, settling down and living happily ever after. However, you're bewildered when the relationship flounders. You spend a whirlwind month or few together and then it tails off. They don't want to settle down or continue. They lack integrity and sometimes disrespect you. While you can agree on stuff that surrounds your interests, you can't agree on how to live your lives emotionally or even together. You seem to want it more than they do. They only seem to want it when you don't.

When you think about letting the fantasy and them go, you think back to the 'hooks'; the shared interests that you've never found someone else that shares, how great they look when their hair flops on their forehead, the fact that they've had the same job for 25 years, have lots of friends (although on closer inspection no actual close friends) and the great sex or sexual tension. 'But we have so much in common!' you think and then you start picturing again, and in your mind you can't imagine anyone more right for you. But they're still resisting being with you, or have even moved onto someone else.

After it's ended you think you won't ever love someone the way that you loved them. Every time you think about moving on, you keep going back to the 'hooks'. You decide that what you have is too good to let go of, so even though they haven't changed, you go back. This may mean both mentally going back to the fantasy and physically attempting to get it, or just holding on mentally and almost hoping that they'll feel compelled to deliver via osmosis.

If you try to make it happen with them, it won't be long before the cracks reappear. You're still picturing though and you're focused on the hooks and how they make the relationship so right and still seeing potential in them and the relationship. You remember what it felt like when you weren't together and then contrast it with how you feel even just pursuing the fantasy of realising their potential, and so remain stuck on the hooks.

The thing is, all this time when you're doing the picturing, you're taking isolated things and breathing life into the image that represents the potential of the relationship, but, ironically, in spite of all of this picturing, you still fail to see the whole picture. If you did, you'd see that you may have these 'hooks', but when it comes to the things that count, like the shared values and mutual love, care, trust and respect, you have very little or nothing to hang the relationship on.

You're looking at the hooks but you're not looking at the wall. They're either hanging on a crumbling wall sitting on poor foundations, or the wall is a mirage.

Here's the reality: You can never know the true potential of your relationship if what you derive the potential from is illusionary or based on things that in the grander scheme of stuff are not that important, and you can certainly can't see potential in a relationship where you're only looking at a partial, convenient view. If you view your relationship or what you see this person as, as the icing on a cake, when you take it off, the cake is hollow, or even rotting. When you inflate someone and the potential for a relationship with them, all of the hot air that you're breathing in leaves no room for substance.

Key Hooks

Status: Position, standing, popularity, fame, money, authority, power. You perceive your status to increase in their presence, so, of course, letting them go will cause you to feel diminished. You're the type of person that will also say stuff like, 'But they're liked by everyone', even though you don't experience the benefit of that 'wonderfulness' you place so much emphasis on.

Security: Money, family, perceived ability to commit, their presence, having a title. You convince yourself that whatever it is that you believe that they bring to the relationship or that you perceive them as holding the power to give you the capability of, that you can't do without them.

Sex & Passion: Drama, spontaneity, excitement, great in bed, sexual chemistry and attraction, 'best you've ever had' syndrome. You're the type of person that could feel hooked on someone and believe they are right for you based on instant attraction or having an orgasm. Even though you may complain about it, you like the up and down of the relationship, the 'drugs' that make you feel like you're on a high. If it wasn't like this, you could unhook yourself without a backward glance.

Plans: They talk about things that they would like to do with you and even when they don't materialise, you feel invested in the relationship because you talked about these plans and you want them to be delivered. It's like, 'Only people who are serious about you talk about plans so they must have been serious about me, so I'm going to make these plans happen because they said so.'

Pain & Problems (Sympathy & Control): Their problems allow you to feel like you're on a pedestal. When you see that they're in pain or have issues, you feel needed and see the opportunity to fix, heal and help. You're hooked on the idea of being their fix-all solution.

Propensity (or lack of) to Commit: You're either eager for commitment and don't really care who it comes from, you just want to be in a relationship. Or... the moment that you realise that they're not commitment material is the more interested and pseudo committed you are. Then it becomes ruminating on why they can't commit and betting on the long-shot of them eventually 'coming good' on your investment.

Disinterest & Rejection: You feel most drawn to a person when their interest isn't returned or they cause you to feel rejected in the relationship. The less they want you, the more convinced you are that you want them.

Appearance: You base your perception of them on superficial stuff that you use as a basis to make assumptions about their suitability as a partner. You're the type of person that could be blinded by beauty. You may bask in the reflected beauty and feel exceptionally desirable and validated, which means when your fantasy isn't fulfilled you feel rejected. Or, you imagine how much more 'technicolor' your life should and would be, if only someone 'like them' would choose you, and then of course feel rejected while at the same time convincing yourself that they're the only person you can be with.

Validation & Righteousness: Positioning yourself in situations where you let yourself be reliant on them for confirmation of your worthiness. Or you're the type of person that likes to be right and will die on your sword trying to prove your rightness rather than leave things be. You're either hooked on being defined by others which means you hand over your power to people who are in no position to be the judge of you, or you're hooked on having the last word.

Interest: They showed you interest so you feel compelled to return it, often feeling near grateful. Of course you may fantasise that because they appeared to show interest in you that your fantasy may be realised and then of course when it isn't, you feel rejected and become hooked on getting back their interest and the future that you thought you'd have.

Connection: Sex, common interests, sense of humour, similar jobs, backgrounds, childhoods. To be honest, you could make a connection out of anything. I've come across readers who have felt connected because their pets died at similar ages, they both liked an obscure film or book, they both laughed at similar things or they've both been afraid of commitment – I kid you not.

Fantasy: Getting caught up in having the relationship in your head. Certain things trigger your propensity to fantasise and get hijacked by your imagination. You get hooked when you really can create something in your head.

Regret: Trapped in blame and shame, you obsess about them and the relationship which is basically looking for reasons to blame yourself for why they don't want you. You play the Coulda, Woulda, Shoulda game and the Let Me Play Grissom or Columbo and investigate the crap out of why it didn't work out and absorb the blame for everything, or put it all on someone else and then regret that I couldn't change them or have done something differently to avoid them or the situation. Then you regret that you spent so much time and energy and feel embarrassed or even ashamed, and so get hooked on that instead.

RUNNING INTO PROBLEMS IN FANTASY LAND

When you experience an issue in the relationship, you try to solve real problems, such as the fact that the relationship isn't working, by making new assumptions that are tied to previous assumptions you've made about qualities, characteristics, and values they possess, while using your picture of the relationship and any potential as the backdrop.

This means that when you're thinking about how to deal with the situation, when you consider how you think they 'should' or 'will' deal with it and how you will deal with it, you formulate your response on dangerous assumptions.

When you're engaging with and trying to get them to understand your point of view or to do whatever it is that you expect, persisting with the assumptions means that it becomes a bit like you're speaking Chinese and they're speaking French, plus at times it will seem like you're talking about an entirely different person and relationship. You then feel frustrated, hurt and confused when, of course, what you thought should and would happen doesn't materialise, no doubt feeling rejected or even abandoned. At this point, you can either keep heaping fantasy coals on your fire, or you can accept the feedback from real life and get conscious, so that you can reconcile the picture of how you see things with the actuality.

BUT THEY'VE CHANGED!

I've had thousands of emails and comments over the years of writing Baggage Reclaim that go along the lines of 'It was so great at the beginning, why can't they go back to being THAT person? Why have they changed?' Let's keep it real here – particularly if you're in the early stages of a relationship, so the first days, weeks and months, they haven't 'changed'; they've revealed who they are.

There's a reason why it's called 'getting to know someone' – it's because you are gaining knowledge about them through observation, asking questions and information. Even if you have observed and asked questions, or gathered some information, you know what? That doesn't mean that that's 'it'. If you observe further things that contradict or change the nature of what you think you know or what you expect, or the answers to questions change, or your ability to ask questions and get answers is impeded, or you gain further information that informs you of what reality is, it's your job to be heeding this feedback, and applying it, even if you don't like it.

When you feel like they've done an about turn on what you thought you knew, it's important to recognise something important: The fact that someone would change so dramatically for you to feel that they've 'changed' is at the very least a code amber, or code red, abort mission. You are far more likely to be put in this position if there were illusions based around what may seem like the most innocuous of assumptions. It's not that they've changed – they're not complying with the image that you've created. You then feel cheated, deceived and robbed.

You don't need an image of person – you just need the real person. Instead of interacting with a static image in your mind that isn't altering to reflect reality, focus on interacting with people in reality where you don't need to have images and blind assumptions.

ASSESSING YOUR HOOKS & LETTING GO OF POTENTIAL

Part of the reason why you're still hooked on the hooks is that they're a mix of fact and fiction and the two have become blurred – you don't know where some things start and others begin. You're struggling to let go because even if it is flimsy, there is some truth in there... you just don't know what it is. Just because there are grains of truth in something though, doesn't make it actually true. You stick around because you hope that how you see things will reveal itself if you just wait around long enough. The pain that you experience is reality piercing the denial bubble.

To start unhooking yourself you need to accept this: You're having a 'relationship', not with the person, but with the image of the relationship that you would like to have. You're not relating to the person because if you were, you would realise that there is a disconnect between your perception of things and reality.

Healthy relationships with a chance of progressing require the two parties to relate to each other. When there are illusions and you're focused on the 'good points' or on insubstantial stuff to the exclusion of seeing the bigger picture, it means that you're actually relating with the images of the relationship and that person, not the actual person.

You can't save a relationship if you're not even trying to save a relationship that exists.

You can't hold onto someone if you're not even trying to hold onto a person that exists.

WHAT YOU THINK MINUS WHAT ACTUALLY ISN'T = **REALITY**

It's not as easy as telling yourself that your relationship was a falsehood – you did experience something (unless you fabricated the whole thing), but you need to get real about what that something was and see what you're left with. At least if you're going to stay or work at a relationship, make sure you're being real about it, because otherwise you're wasting time. That and if you're going to work at a relationship, there has to be another party working there right alongside you. At least if you're going to be interested in someone and want a relationship with them, ensure that it's for solid reasons that directly apply to your interaction with them and benefit the relationship, not just in the short-term, but in the medium-term and beyond. You will find that the moment that you apply actions that in essence amount to responsibility, accountability, and honesty, your fantasy relationship can no longer exist.

TAKE THE RELATIONSHIP OUT OF YOUR HEAD AND PUT IT DOWN ON PAPER

One of the things that makes a fantasy relationship so 'unreal' is that it doesn't get taken out of your head and, often, friends and family have no idea what you're up to so it's not like you're sanity checking your thoughts and ideas. Instead, all of this stuff goes round and round and round, in much the same way that many people who don't address their issues have their thoughts knocking around unprocessed.

List all the reasons why you love this person, why you want them, why you stay/stayed, why even if they're gone you can't let go of them and go through them one by one and ask yourself what is true, exaggerated, non-existent or over-weighted. Remove what is untrue, reassess and re-describe anything that is exaggerated and over-weighted and acknowledge what you haven't got out of the relationship.

What did you think would happen (potential) in the relationship? What has actually happened and what is the difference between the two? The reality of your relationship – can you work with this? Or does it amount to crumbs?

Some tips:
Anything that you regard as being 'true' must be something that has been consistently demonstrated by them or experienced in your interaction. Stick to what is factual, indisputable and not contradicted by other qualities, characteristics, values and experiences. Anything you go

on about them being to other people, must be something that you know to be true directly to you. Authentic people don't roll out different personalities for different people.

To work out what has been exaggerated, you likely only have to look at what you emphasise the most. When you talk or think about them, what do you keep harping on about? If you forced yourself to be on equal footing and evaluated your own positive attributes, would they really be so great? It's also safe to say that there's exaggeration going on if the things that you think are so great about them are things that you yourself are missing or don't recognise your own capability in.

Does anything you regard as true contradict something else you know about them? If it's untrue, the existence of the other factors negates it. If it's not untrue, but is contradictory, its existence is either exaggerated or the importance of it in and to your relationship is over-weighted. You can get a very good idea of what is truly important to your relationship by the problems that you're experiencing. Often, when you think that you have so much in common, it is superficial stuff that isn't anywhere near as pertinent as the things that prevent this relationship from actually taking shape and working.

How did you want to feel in the relationship? Write down how you thought you'd feel about yourself, a relationship, them, love, the universe, or even your past. What positive emotions did you expect to feel? Which feelings did you think would change and to what level? For instance, if you were unhappy, what level of happiness did you expect to go from and to? For example, 'I expected to go from a level 2/10 unhappiness to a 9.' Why did you expect these feelings or expect these changes? Put down your reasons no matter how small.

How did you actually feel? Taking the list of how you wanted to feel, with 1 being the least accurate and 10 being the most accurate, take each item on your list and rate it.

These feelings, are they based on them or on the image of the type of relationship you'd like to have but aren't actually having? This is the fantasy.

It's also good to compare the person with the positive and negative characteristics and qualities of people like your parents or even ex partners – you may be trying to recreate feelings with partners based on old patterns which give you familiarity and possibly an opportunity to right the wrongs from your past.

At the end of the day, whatever you have left, did you have a relationship with mutual love, care, trust and respect with shared values and boundaries?

Whatever love you feel/felt, was it reciprocated? Whatever care you have given, did they give it? Whatever trust you had, did they show themselves to be trustworthy and did they trust you? Whatever respect you gave, whatever admiration and even adulation, did you get it back? Write down live examples – don't try to match your fantasy actions with their fantasy actions. Stick with evidence.

All of the things that you see and feel about this person and the relationship, were they manifested in front of your eyes? Can you see them? Can you hear them? Can you touch them, and not just occasionally but if you need to reach out and touch, can this be done there without barriers? Can you smell your relationship? Or do you just smell bullshit?

After you've worked out the facts and deducted your own fantasy, if you're left with very little of substance, it's safe to say that whatever's holding you there is a major sign that you're focusing on very insubstantial things to the exclusion of what is needed for a healthy, sustainable relationship.

SANITY CHECK YOUR HOOK AS A VALUE

People have said to me, 'But what if the hook is true or is a value?' For a start, it depends on what the hook is. Anything can be true but it doesn't make it right for your relationship. Telling me it's true he was a great lay, very important, kind to animals, wanted to get married is all well and good, but if he was a great lay, very important, not that kind to you, and didn't actually want to get married whether it's because he verbally stated it or made sure it didn't happen via his actions, there's just no point in talking about it. They're overvalued.

Aside from mutual love, care, trust, respect plus the landmarks of a healthy relationship, commitment, progression, intimacy, consistency and balance, the only things that should 'hook' you to a relationship in conjunction with the former, are shared values.

Whatever values you profess to have, you don't realise that your hooks are telling you what it is that you truly value and this actually presents you with an opportunity to have a clear-out and align yourself with the values you profess to have that should be paving the way to living your life authentically, instead of being distracted by the 'glitter' of the hooks.

For every hook that has kept you in this or any previous relationship, it's time to ask yourself: **What has this hook done for me lately?**

Is it a quality, characteristic or value that you yourself are living by?

Is it what you believe to be a core, primary value and, if so, is this something that you can actually say out loud, whether it's to you or a third party, that this is fundamental to your happiness and living your life authentically?

I value _____ and it's fundamentally important to my life, happiness and wellbeing. Without it, it doesn't matter what else I do, I would not be living my life authentically and I'd feel unhappy, unfulfilled or even downright miserable.

Most of the things that hook people to unhealthy relationships look downright ridiculous when put into the context of values.

For me, unhooking myself was initially a daily act in denying myself the act of bullshitting me. Bad enough that someone else would lie to me, but to grieve the loss of my relationship so that I could move on, I made sure I had an honest conversation with myself and went on a Bullshit Diet.

It is making a conscious effort and choice, not to accept every waking thought, assumption, desire, and belief as fact, right, or necessary.

It was tough at first because, when you're used to bullshitting yourself, the truth can be highly unpalatable, but every time I became nostalgic and felt the pull of the 'experiences' and 'feelings' that I had images of, I replaced them with a reality image. When I remembered my feelings of love for him and how he told me that he was 'crazy about me' and that nobody would or could love me like he did, it was painful to admit that, as he hadn't actually left his girlfriend, hence we never actually in the relationship I wanted or that he claimed we had, plus between the two of us, I hadn't been treated very well, the reality was that whatever his version of love was, it wasn't enough, plus it didn't look or feel like love – it felt like pain.

When I decided to be more 'present', I didn't just let myself run riot and get hijacked by my imagination – you have to be accountable for everything that you think or imagine about this person and force yourself to see them and the relationship as they are, which might be none at all.

It's not up to them to prove your fantasy right – it's up to you to be working with a realistic vision and putting your effort into a real relationship in the first place because you are accountable and responsible for anything that you decide to latch on to and make the basis of your thought process and subsequent decisions.

You deserve reality... and so do they. If unhooking yourself means letting go of them and the relationship because the reality cannot work for you, at least you're free to get into a real relationship rather than clutching at the straws of insubstantial hooks.

ACHILLES HEEL: REJECTION AVOIDANCE

There are two key things that everyone desires and fears in life; acceptance and rejection, and without one, you have the other. An area of life that you cannot avoid experiencing some level of 'rejection' is dating and relationships, because not all dates and relationships are supposed to work out. Short of only ever being with one person, you will have to turn people down, let go and break up with them and vice versa. It's unavoidable and being able to say NO, to opt out of situations, to admit when something isn't working, is part of the natural order of freeing yourself up to be available for a mutual relationship. Unfortunately, all Fallback Girls have some major issues with rejection, either taking it too hard and being derailed by it, or busting a gut to ensure that they don't experience it. As a Dreamer, you are so afraid of rejection, you have withdrawn into a fantasy bubble.

If you place yourself in situations that make it difficult to be fully 'rejected', you've got a serious case of **Rejection Avoidance.** This means attempting to avoid being turned down, discovering that your feelings aren't reciprocated, that you're not 'good enough', or that the relationship isn't working or has even ended. What better place to do this but in a fantasy relationship or any relationship that in essence represents the long shot and which you've already accepted failure at anyway?

You take rejection very personally and it can totally distort your view of yourself because you love you conditionally, and you've never learned how to cope with rejection because you never accept what has happened, grieve the loss with perspective, and move forward.

Symptoms

'What's wrong with me?' 'What did I do?' 'I'm not good enough' is your internal dialogue.

Have a tendency to perceive all things that don't go your way as 'rejection'.

Persistently think about the 'rejection' even when you claim you're not.

Take a disproportionately long period of time to get over someone — it could take months to get over someone you knew for a few short weeks or even days.

Stewing and ruminating on a breakup for such a long time because you persist in reopening the wound, throwing salt on it and revisiting prior rejections that in truth you haven't gotten over either.

Afraid of abandonment.

May have been abandoned as a child, adopted or bounced around the foster care system.

Lost a parent to death but felt abandoned, particularly if you ended up being mistreated or sidelined.

Never fully grieve the loss of your relationships.

Bullied or found it very difficult to 'fit in' at school.

Numb from burying your feelings as a coping mechanism.

Can feel isolated as you can't see past your feelings.

May be so hyper-sensitive to rejection that you may deem disagreements, or others not doing things in the manner in which you would expect, as rejection.

Likely to do disappearing acts, especially when you think the relationship is in danger.

Will profess your feelings and then say you were joking.

Will lie low and then test the waters with an email or text. Even a minor response lets you feel 'accepted', albeit temporarily.

Have a near compulsive urge to make contact whenever you come close to accepting that it's over/they're not interested.

Won't admit how you feel but may hint and/or lurk.

Feelings intensify when you know they're not interested or want out.

May believe it's not a full rejection as long as you still believe you have a chance, even if they've said otherwise.

Limit the contact and interaction – long-distance relationships, avoiding meeting up, imagining more to a relationship with an infrequent visitor.

May have long periods of not dating or declare celibacy.

Bargainer – may water down a relationship to a bare existence including booty call / hookup to avoid rejection.

Have a parent, caregiver, or even an ex who was an addict or had serious issues that as a result of their failure to change or love you as you would have liked, is taken as a great rejection.

All this time when you've been dodging rejection, you don't realise what you've been doing – rejecting yourself.

The very things that you're going to such painstaking efforts to avoid are basically acts of rejecting yourself before anyone else has a chance to do it, while also living a half-life because you're tied up in fear. From not loving and liking yourself, to having little or no boundaries, to repeatedly going back to the relationship crime scene, to living in a fantasy bubble, to morphing and adapting, to putting a fantasy or some upstart of a man's needs above your own, these are all acts of self-rejection. While you may rationalise that all of these things are still not as bad as what you fear out and out rejection would be like, it's like six of one, half a dozen of another.

When you contemplate rejection, it resurrects an old and unresolved prior 'rejection'.

As you've never dealt with the original rejection, avoiding the pain is about attempting to avoid going 'back there' but experiencing even slight rejection can resurrect the pain which you have all stored up, simmering away. You quickly slam the proverbial lid shut on your feelings but it's too late – you know that these feelings are there, so even though you're not fully experiencing the full-on rejection that you fear, just being aware of the presence of them can eat away at you. It's like peeking inside Pandora's Box. They'll likely niggle as well, making it harder to keep a lid on them, which may prompt you to quickly find some relief by burying yourself into some fantasising. In turn, this also helps to push these feelings back into the box but they're always trying to jostle their way out and ultimately, they're still there.

Since the original rejection, you've experienced other perceived rejections which have only exacerbated your fears. These are all blurred in with the original rejection and act as shields to the old hurt. It can be one of the reasons why you find it very difficult to get over a relationship, even if it seems like it was for a very short time or was actually less serious than a previous relationship that lasted much longer but took you a shorter period of time to get over. This hurt will sting and stick in your craw because not only did you have a lot invested in this particular person/relationship, but the loss of it and the judgement you've subsequently made about you has left you bereft – you've lost them and yourself.

Due to these feelings that you're trying to stuff down and avoid, you're not only highly sensitive to the possibility of rejection but by being so hyper vigilant, you end up feeling rejection even when you're not actually experiencing rejection.

When you think about what avoiding something involves, you realise that it involves an awful lot of effort and can end up, as a result of deselecting yourself from potential opportunities to confront what you seek to avoid, shutting out the good too. The person who avoids going out for fear of something 'bad' happening, ends up with an even greater of fear of leaving their home and due to the fact that that they don't go out and they haven't addressed what is at the root of their fear, just thinking about going out can send them into a tailspin. Of course as a result of not going out, any attempts to do so will be terrifying and they'll be highly sensitive to stepping out.

It's the same with dating, intimacy, and ultimately putting yourself out there and being vulnerable – the more you avoid, the greater the distance between your last experience of actually doing these things, is the greater the level of anxiety experienced, is the heightened sense of needing to avoid.

You 'choose' people that reflect your beliefs and the 'marks' you choose are actually more carefully chosen than you realise – men that you know are not going to reciprocate or are unlikely to, or relationships that offer the least likely chance of actually amounting to anything and putting you in the position of truly being vulnerable, and ultimately situations that you know are a long-shot and keep you in your comfort zone. Mr Unavailables, especially ones that don't tax you too much and rely on distance between you, are perfect for rejection avoidance.

Like I've said throughout the book – you could try with someone that's available, but it's like any vague hopes of not being rejected are based around trying to obtain acceptance from a reluctant source, which is quite frankly, a bit fucked up. However, the likelihood is that Mr Unavailable has some qualities, characteristics and behaviours that also remind you of where you experienced your old rejection so, of course, there's an element of righting the wrongs of the past so you can 'win'. In some instances, you've 'given up' on yourself, so someone like him or the fantasy is a last resort and, yet, you still end up being hurt.

Your fear of rejection means that being with an available partner isn't on the cards because, for you, rejection doesn't feel quite as bad as you imagine it would with someone that you believe is more worthy but that who you're not convinced that you're worthy of, so either way, whether it's from others or from you, you manage to find rejection at every turn.

The stage has been set and you're sticking to the script, a script and a play that you've written, produced, directed and acted in.

That's your self-fulfilling prophecy at work and you ultimately can't feel 'full rejection', or even abandonment when you predicted that it would happen, because all you're doing is confirming what you felt would happen while putting salt on the wound and almost getting comfort out of the pain.

Your rejection formula is all an illusion anyway, because yes, while you can convince yourself that what you're experiencing isn't as bad as what it could be if you were truly putting yourself out there, you just don't know this – what are you measuring it against? A past experience that if you recognised the growth you can attain from it, that you'd be more than equipped to handle now because you're not that person anymore, or at least you don't have to be if you choose not to be. Does what you're thinking, feeling, and experiencing really look like a better option to you? And, let's not forget, you're experiencing rejection anyway and you are being greatly impacted by it to such an extent that you are withdrawing inwardly. This isn't what 'safe' and 'better' looks like.

Rejection, like conflict, is unavoidable.

You experience it in subtle and not so subtle ways in all facets of life. Not everything can go our way, it's impossible for everyone to like and love us, situations and feelings change, and people aren't always what they say on the tin. To expect to date and have relationships and experience no rejection, is quite frankly incredibly unrealistic and this is what sets you up for a fall.

You're avoiding something that's unavoidable, which means you're burning up precious energy that could be better used to improve your self-esteem and to learn to handle the nos that come with life.

Fact is, you're not the only one experiencing it – everyone is or has at some point, and will again in one guise or another, and by opting out of and avoiding rejection by basically never truly being in something or out of it, for it to 'count' as a 'full rejection', is actually robbing you of the opportunity to not only learn to love yourself by nurturing and supporting you when you do experience rejection, but also robbing you of being available for an available relationship and for your own life.

ACHILLES HEEL: GREAT EXPECTATIONS

If everybody made a point of thinking about what their expectations are and expressing them, relationships would improve drastically. If Fallback Girls evaluated theirs and then expressed them to Mr Unavailables, and then computed the information and did something with the knowledge, there'd be no such thing as Fallback Girls. If you as a Dreamer tempered your expectations with reality, which means the reality of your own actions and beliefs, his, plus the circumstances, you wouldn't be so led by your fantasies.

Great expectations is about unexpressed and unevaluated too high and too low expectations that arise out of a very unrealistic view of relationships. Two factors impact hugely on your expectations: your idea of unconditional love and your own self-hate or self-dislike. One person consumed by these two things that totally negate one another creates a clash of mixed ideals that have no real basis. You effectively paint yourself into a corner and tie yourself up in knots, and due to your beliefs, it will feed into a vicious cycle of a self-fulfilling prophecy as you remain in your comfort zone.

The fantasy vision of a relationship, and what you believe it 'should' look and feel like, can be a mix of feelings you want the other person to create in you, qualities, characteristics and values you might assume, righting the wrongs of the past with your imagination where you both be and do all the things that you feel should have happened in the past, as well as intermingling with things that represent your pattern that you've grown accustomed to. Unevaluated and depending on where you're drawing all of this inspiration from, you end up being and feeling conflicted in search of something that doesn't exist, or trying to get it from inappropriate sources.

Symptoms

Expectation paralysis – you're suspended in expectation, obsessing about what 'should' and 'could' and 'would' be, if only...

Feel that you've never been loved or have been loved conditionally.

Parent made you work for their love and were often disparaging.

Been in an abusive relationship.

Very focused on companionship.

Avoid facing the truth about people.

See his problems (real or imagined) as the obstacle, not him.

Often feel desperate and may have contemplated or even attempted suicide.

Have to medicate to cope with breakups or being alone.

Feel that people rarely give to you and that they abuse your generosity.

Don't know how to say no, so may be an indispensable over-giver.

Think couples should be together all the time.

Anxious even when he's away temporarily.

Often won't question his behaviour for fear of him not coming back.

Believe that love conquers all.

Can be emotionally demanding often because your expectations greatly exceed the reality of your relationship.

Think people and relationships are there to 'fill you up' and make you whole.

Look to everyone and anyone for validation and become pissed off when you don't get it or feel 'rejected'.

Love to generalise. 'People should...' and 'If it were me...'

Passive aggressive – can appear to be complying but are actually working to your agenda of trying to have your expectations met, even if you've been told they won't be.

Inclined to focus on complaining about the problem, rather than solving it.

May fall out with friends and family over your ideas of what you think that they should be doing for you.

Still waiting for a parent to say the magic words you've been waiting for all of your life.

Consider yourself to be optimistic, but depending on how much fantasising you do, you can be hopeful to the point of being deluded.

Inadvertently believe that your feelings and hopes for someone and the relationship exist because they're an indicator of the possibilities and entitlement to a relationship.

Dreamers, in particular, overcompensate for the lack of input from the outset of the 'relationship', because he's either quite ambivalent and a bit take it or leave it, or he's not even aware of the level of relationship and connection that is being assumed and expected.

Mr Unavailables tend to believe, even if they have led you to think otherwise, that you expect less than you do, simply because how they see things is less than you do anyway. That and there is some very contradictory actions and/or words taking place that they use as their get out clause because they think you've got the 'hint'.

Unfortunately, any expectations that you have of him and the relationship aren't growing because the relationship is growing and he's demonstrating his capabilities; they're growing because the volume of giving, fantasising and self-hate is on the rise.

All Fallback Girls look to love and be loved unconditionally without knowing what it means – loving and staying true to you regardless of what's taking place externally. It doesn't mean loving without limits, nor does it mean trying to make someone love you that can't or doesn't, and it certainly doesn't mean accepting even the crappiest of behaviour that violates you. It's also impossible to claim to love someone else unconditionally if you love you conditionally; yet this is exactly what Fallback Girls do every day. You apply no conditions to him and plenty to yourself and then add on your expectations. To make this even more complex, when you then add a fantasy element, it's the perfect opportunity to have no limits (it's your imagination after all) and to attempt to experience unconditional love.

The problem is that these expectations and illusions do have a condition that you can't escape no matter how hard you try – reality.

Sometimes you under-expect. When this happens, it's because you believe that it's what you deserve or that you can't do better (another fantasy), and this will draw in people that cater to these beliefs. It's also because sometimes, when you don't want to expect too much of people, it's because you don't want them to expect too much of you. Unfortunately while they may deliver to your level of under expectation, if you have little or no boundaries and are not aware of what you're communicating about yourself, or how you can be taken advantage of or abused, you'll have people who will even manage to under-deliver on your meagre expectations, which will of course scream, 'I'm not good enough!' You may also find that you coast along through life in a near coma of disappointment and frustration.

Ultimately, under-expecting is accepting failure and poor results from the outset. You lower your expectations to be in a state of not being disappointed.

When you over-expect, you're setting yourself up to be disappointed and to fail, because you are unrealistic. You believe that people who want to be around or with you, should meet your lofty expectations because you have some preconceived ideas that haven't been sanity checked. You'll communicate that you're high-maintenance, emotionally demanding, and possibly controlling, but you'll also communicate that your head is in the clouds because you don't come back down to earth and adjust your expectations – you just assume that people should meet them and when they don't, they feel the wrath of your disappointment. Sometimes, you have high expectations because you don't want people to get too close in case they discover the perceived flaws that you hide behind the bravado.

Ultimately, over-expecting also accepts failure from the outset – it's a mix of 'optimism' laced with the expectation of disappointment.

'Unconditional love' is one of the most overused terms that gives women carte blanche to be absolved from having to choose a decent man and be responsible for their decisions. Hard to hear but true. Between focusing your feelings, expectations and the imagined relationship in his direction and having little or no basis for all this energy you're expending, you're creating one-way traffic. Regardless of whether you're a Dreamer or in another Fallback role, and regardless of whether it's 'real' or a 'fantasy', there's always one particular expectation that's held by Fallback Girls:

You all believe that eventually there will be a tipping point of all this expenditure of energy, emotions and fantasising and that you'll be matched.

Now, you've already seen how problematic this can be, but can you imagine (excuse the pun) where it's mostly or all fantasy, where really the limits are the boundaries of your imagination, how dangerous this can be?

When the rude awakening from your expectations and imagining happens, it can feel incredibly painful and overwhelming, which may force you to retreat, become defensive and go on the offensive, or even harm yourself. Even when there's a relationship there, many Fallback Girls find it difficult to admit that not only have they made a mistake but that they had excessive expectations and may in fact insist that they're 'right', while he's 'wrong'. Either way, this only suffices to make it even harder to get over the relationship, plus if you don't accept that there's too much imagination and expectation and not enough reality, you'll just lather, rinse, repeat with the same expectations in a new relationship or feel cheated by the dating pool: 'There's no decent men to date! I'm destined to be alone!'

It is the excessive expectations and the hopes, dreams, fantasies, plans and any real life activities based around them, that have you struggling to grieve the loss of a relationship... even though it wasn't actually a relationship or it wasn't representative of all of the expectations that you had. Getting over a relationship that didn't exist or has a large element of illusions, is actually in some respects harder than your atypical breakup. You have to get over yourself and grieve the loss of all of the hopes, dreams etc to get back to base – reality.

Great expectations in relationships without the appropriate foundations including love, trust, and commitment means that you're removing conditions to both of your contributions, and in effect, removing accountability. That, and you cannot hold him accountable to expectations that are based on your imagination and the potential you envision. You might of course argue that what you expect is 'normal' and in part it may be... if you were with a healthy partner, but expecting indiscriminately from your relationships without thought for your own capacity, never mind theirs, is to ultimately end up catering to your unhealthy and unrealistic   beliefs.

THE KNOCK-ON EFFECT

The trouble with loving, admiring, crushing and all manner of emotional expenditure from a distance, is that while it helps you to avoid rejection and go through the motions of attempting to meet your great expectations, it ultimately triggers a knock-on effect that removes other components that are needed for healthy relationships, while heightening related fears. You cannot avoid fundamental components of life and a relationship and expect to get a great relationship with bells and whistles, or even a barely decent one. All of the things you avoid and are afraid of are like neon invitations and gravitational pulls for unhealthy interactions. When you avoid rejection and have distorted expectations, you also engage in intimacy, rejection, criticism, conflict, and abandonment avoidance, as well building up a pattern of relating and coping that lets you remain in control of your experiences. Find out how over the next few chapters.

AVOIDING REJECTION LEADS TO
AVOIDING INTIMACY

There's an illusion of intimacy that surrounds unavailable relationships, because it's often feigned through sped-up connections, synergy over emotional discord in your respective pasts, a quiet recognition that they fit your pattern, latching onto crumbs and not really knowing what intimacy is – being vulnerable, emotionally engaged and risking one's self in order to be truly emotionally open and committed.

When I say 'risk' I don't mean running around doing unhealthy stuff and taking gambles on people who you know, even if you deny it, cannot love you or are unwilling to be in a mutual relationship.

Risk means that you opt into life in spite of the fact that there's a possibility that sometimes you'll be disappointed or even unhappy if something doesn't pan out.

Conversely, it also means you get to experience the positive flip side if you don't spend your time, emotion and energy in and on situations that detract from you. This means that while you'll still be disappointed or even sad on occasion, the incidences for this shrink dramatically when you live, date and love with your self-esteem in tow.

Instead, you're afraid of the consequences of being so emotionally vulnerable that for it not to work out would hurt – you don't want to run

121

the risk so you put up walls and limit yourself in unavailable relationships.

By putting up walls and accepting failure from the outset, due to your beliefs and relationships habits, you accept that there's inevitably going to be hurt, while being super-optimistic in the height of your fantasy, so as a result you limit the amount of hurt you experience by catering to the self-fulfilling prophecy and playing with 'known' dangers. If the risk pays off (which it won't) it's like a massive bonus reward, but if it doesn't, it's no more than you expected anyway.

You've also mistaken being vulnerable and risking one's self in relationships as betting on potential and taking a punt on a three-legged horse relationship. Being vulnerable and risking yourself is confused with feeling attraction and charging in, regardless of distinct warning signs that all is not well. If you're the type that shuts out anything that contradicts the fantasy, it's like jumping into a pool of sharks with a blindfold, ears blocked and your brain in sleep mode.

Letting go of the illusion of intimacy that you experience in these relationships means that you can recognise where you're shortchanging yourself. Without intimacy, you cannot be emotionally available, including emotionally honest, or committed.

You're either in or you're out – half in or three-quarters in, or ten percent in, is out.

When you're prepared to feel all of your feelings, aside from helping you to be honest and available, it also means that you go in consciously and make more informed choices and decisions. This isn't to say that you might not get hurt at some point, but you will recover.

RESPONSIBILITY? WHAT'S THAT?

There's no such thing as a life or a relationship or even a personal experience without responsibility. All this dodging rejection and fantasising is causing you to take your hands off the wheel of your own life. The thing is, if you want to experience mutual love, care, trust, respect, commitment and intimacy, responsibility comes as a fundamental part of the package. You have to continue being responsible for yourself and be responsible for your relationship.

Mutual relationships involve you working together for a positive outcome – if you both dodge responsibility like a hot potato, you just cannot be committed to your relationship. You need to commit to reality, to your thoughts and feelings, to the impact of your actions and ensuring that what you say matches what you do – this is what responsibility looks like. You've got to meet your own obligations and take full control of you so that you can have responsibility for your life.

You have a duty to you. Dodging responsibility by dreaming away your life and waiting for someone and an opportunity to rescue you, will leave you feeling like you've been cast back out to a life and a you that you don't want when things don't work out.

Your serious fear of failure, rejection, making and admitting mistakes, also removes the accountability and responsibility in your life. You cannot have the glory of success without the responsibility or the experience of the mistakes along the way.

Commitment doesn't happen without intimacy, and it's impossible to have intimacy without responsibility.

The lack of willingness to fully commit and be vulnerable enough to be responsible for one's actions, the impact of them, and any mistakes that happen along the way, is a fundamental reason why unavailable relationships prevail – neither one of you want the responsibility. Each time it gets too much, one or both of you do things to take things back to each of your respective Status Quo's, which ultimately meets each of your respective self-fulfilling prophecies.

Whether you're blaming yourself or blaming others for how your life is, what you're not doing is taking responsibility for your life. You're assigning 'responsibility' but you're not taking any, nor are you being realistic about what you're apportioning blame about. You're even a perfectionist about blame – you either assume all of the blame and absolve the other person of the reality of their actions, or you offload all of the blame and assume the role of helpless victim.

Blame is not the same as responsibility. Blame is actually responsibility dodging.

If when you're faced with taking action in your life, you come up with an excuse as to why you don't make it happen, or at least attempt to, you are lessening the responsibility that you have for your life. These excuses may appear to be real reasons but what they ultimately do is allow you to remain in an uncomfortable comfort zone where avoidance and fantasy reside. If you're not moving to plan B or C after making an excuse for why you're not evolving and moving forward, you can be sure that they're not genuine reasons because when they are, there's a solution or at least the beginnings of one in the offing. When you make excuses, you accept 'defeat' even if you haven't really tried – you find that when you're willing to truly be responsible, you won't make excuses, nor accept them from others.

Accepting responsibility for your life isn't a golden opportunity to find a new reason to punish yourself – it means that if you don't want to continue finding yourself in the same situations and feeling the same way, you've got to start doing things very differently. You don't need a perfect life, not least because it doesn't exist – what you need is a life that you occupy.

STRUGGLING WITH CRITICISM &

CONFLICT

When you struggle to admit mistakes, you also have a thing about being 'right', which is the surefire indicator, along with dodging conflict, that you cannot handle criticism, which is what appears to be an expression of disapproval based on what also appears to be faults, mistakes, or even 'flaws'.

To you, hearing something that you don't like, having a concern expressed or a mistake highlighted, or what appears to be the onset of conflict, are all equivalent to rejection, so you see yourself being disapproved of and 'not up to standard' as soon as things don't appear to be going your way. Due to your sensitivity surrounding it, which may stem from childhood like mine did, you may compromise yourself to pre-empt conflict, or to end conflict, or just get very defensive which may involve telling them all about themselves, or bailing.

I make a point of saying 'appears' – you have a heightened criticism reflex due to your various fears and experiences, specifically avoiding rejection and 'mistakes'.

This means that you can see criticism on the horizon if a text or email isn't responded to as quickly as you'd like, or when you experience discontent and unhappiness about your hopes and expectations not being fulfilled. Whether you silence yourself or make a vague attempt at communicating

126

your feelings, you're already braced for and expecting criticism which likely affects your demeanour and the content of your message.

You don't believe you're good enough so of course you fear and expect criticism. You're also your worst critic.

There are things that you're hung up on about you that you regard as 'faults' or even 'flaws' that have you taking a less than equal position in relationships, so you, like most Fallback Girls, have a tendency to roll yourself out like a doormat to compensate for these 'awful' (they're really not and may even be imagined or at least greatly exaggerated) things, so that you can ward off criticism before it even strikes. Of course this is where you can run into trouble as there's an expectation that isn't communicated:

That in exchange for you being ever-accommodating and bending your boundaries, you won't be criticised or experience the indicators of it. You also hope that it will ward off conflict, after all, when someone is willing to take a 'less than' position and put up with some rinky dink behaviour, you'd think the least that they could do is not find fault with you and love you.

On the mistake front, while you veer between avoiding mistakes or taking them so much to heart that you fear trying again at putting yourself out there, you often feel that you've made 'mistakes' for fairly innocuous stuff, or latch onto things to blame yourself for the relationship ending, even though you don't see the bigger picture of the fundamental 'mistake' in your thinking and choices in being with them in the first place. This ties back into avoiding responsibility by focusing on blame, when you could be taking responsibility for your choices and changing.

I've heard from so many people who are extremely sensitive to criticism who experienced a breakup after a conflict. The conflict, 99.9% of the time was warranted and in a relationship where each person was being accountable and responsible, when things had calmed down, they would have been able to work through the disagreement and move on. Instead, they broke up and all of these people believe that because they raised valid concerns, or asked questions, and yes, even criticised during the conflict and received it, that this is the reason why the relationship failed. They all believe that if they'd avoided conflict, or not been and done something that warranted criticism, or not themselves found fault in the other, they'd be together riding around in their magical kingdom on a white horse.

And there's something else you can learn about your difficulty handling criticism and conflict – there's no point trying to grit your teeth, bust up your boundaries, ask no questions, silence your needs, apologise fast, accept all the blame etc, in the hope that by avoiding what you think is criticising someone, that you won't experience it yourself. In LaLa Land, there's no criticism or conflict – in reality, there is.

Your great expectations also ensure that in your world, if someone truly loves you, then you won't experience conflict or criticism, or when you do, it'll be all hearts, flowers, and Care Bears. They'll communicate the criticism in a 'perfect' way (you've likely discovered that there's no great way to hear what you don't want to hear anyway) or you'll fight in a perfect way, and you'll then feel certain things, share a warm embrace and a passionate kiss, or rip each other's clothes off and have a glass of champagne afterwards. Whatever your vision of criticism and conflict looks like, it's just not realistic and it sets you up for disappointment.

For you, experiencing criticism (or what appears to be) and conflict when you've been fantasising, is akin to being doused with cold water. It may just be a difference of opinion, or their own feelings about themselves which you're taking on too much of, or very genuine concerns on either side, but it stirs up uncomfortable feelings for you or even reopens an old wound. The illusion bubble bursts and uncomfortable feelings like disappointment and rejection creep in.

It may even transport you back to being a certain age and next thing, you're not really listening or engaging; you're panicking inside or experiencing fury. Suddenly, the possibilities you foresaw for a relationship with them begin to recede rapidly. You may feel like they've 'ruined' things or that you have, and it's the beginning of the end, as you panic about more 'flaws' being discovered, or 'suddenly' start seeing theirs.

You may be planning your escape route or go into overdrive apologising for yourself, with the latter immediately communicating to Mr Unavailable that you're a little too eager to designate him as your expert authority. Maybe you lash out defensively which means in the aftermath you'll focus on the fact that you lashed out and then blame yourself, becoming blinded to the fact that regardless, there were issues. Whatever you do, you respond in your default mode to criticism and conflict, which is unlikely to be rooted in the current, specific incident and is instead responding to old messaging and fears.

Giving and receiving criticism plus experiencing conflict is unavoidable, but it does require maturity on both sides. I can tell you from personal experience – I had to stop seeing my mother every time I got into an argument or experienced criticism because storming off and saying things that left me feeling embarrassed couldn't continue. I had to be prepared to listen and not assume that there was an attack, or that I wasn't good enough, but I also had to be prepared to stake my own claim in my life and needs, which meant that I had to learn to express my disapproval also.

At 28, I discovered that the sky doesn't fall in with criticism or conflict plus you can experience greater intimacy and grow out of them because you're communicating with one another on a level and not being rejected for doing so. I also discovered that in mutually respectful relationships of all kinds, not just romantic, that while it's never easy to hear what may be negative feedback from someone we love, respect, or care about, it's only in unhealthy relationships where criticism doesn't cut both ways. You'll also find, that like honesty, criticism and conflict don't feel like rejection when done with respect and your self-esteem in tow.

FEAR OF ABANDONMENT

For many unavailable people, fear of rejection and the unhealthy expectations that can be held alongside it, are tied up in a fear of abandonment.

When you **fear being abandoned,** it's about being afraid of letting someone get close enough to you that if they weren't around, it would hurt. It's also about the fear of the consequences of conflict because you will be afraid that it (conflict) will result in you realising your fear of abandonment.

For you, the Dreamer, when things don't work out, you feel abandoned by them and the cosy confines of your fantasy. It also reopens old abandonment wounds that you still haven't come to terms with, so it can be like reliving the hurt all over again, even though, if for instance you experienced abandonment in childhood, this is very different to experiencing disinterest or a breakup. It's this lumping rejection and abandonment together that actually heightens your fear of it – everything that you don't like that hints of not being accepted, criticism, conflict or the relationship not working out starts to look and feel like abandonment.

This means that with your great expectations and fantasising, you can build up a person and the possibility of a relationship with them to such a great extent that when they don't reciprocate your feelings, or are not living up to your hopes and expectations, you feel abandoned... even when you may not even know them.

You can feel abandoned when an ex moves on, when a booty call or Friends With Benefits situation ends because they want to move on/don't want to 'upgrade' you, or when the married/attached guy won't leave. It may be that you feel abandoned when friends are not able to drop everything to tend to your latest romantic crisis or, when after morphing and adapting to try to be what you think someone wants while busting up your boundaries in the process, they end up not wanting you anyway. It then becomes, 'Look at all of the things I've done in the name of loving and winning you – how can you leave me like this? What the eff am I supposed to do now? This is all for you – how can you reject it?'

This great fear of being abandoned is what makes fantasising so attractive – technically, how you see things isn't real, even with elements of reality in there, so you can't be truly abandoned by something that hasn't started, or doesn't exist, or that you're not fully opted into.

In spite of your fear of abandonment, you still continue to attempt to date or have relationships, even if you're still very heavily invested in a fantasy. You venture out again on a validation-seeking quest – you invariably seek out people who on some level you recognise tick your unavailable boxes and then end up having your self-fulfilling prophecy catered to. On one hand you hope to challenge your beliefs and get confirmation that you're a loveable person worthy of not being abandoned, but, on the other hand, you will inadvertently seek confirmation that the beliefs you hold about being abandoned are actually true, otherwise you'd have no legitimate reason to keep believing the negative beliefs.

If you're afraid of taking the risk, you'll limit the opportunity to take the risk and rely on the 'safe bet' of limited relationships with people that have limited capacity. This is 'limited hurt' – you're not stretching yourself and taking a healthy risk. Yep, the long shot mentality and accepting failure from the outset strikes again.

The self-fulfilling prophecy is about predicting what you believe is likely to happen. If, at the heart of it, you have negative beliefs, you'll predict in line with those beliefs and act in line with them, so that your prediction becomes a reality. You're prepared for the eventual pain and loss that will no doubt ensue by choosing partners that tick the boxes for your beliefs and relationship pattern. You expect to be abandoned, or should I say rejected, because you don't believe that you're good enough for anyone to stick around.

Let's be real, you also expect to be abandoned because you keep dabbling with the same situations and type – you just hope one will make you the exception to the rule.

When you believe what you believe, especially the more hidden beliefs working overtime underneath, you'd be amazed at what you will do to keep believing – it's familiar and comfortable pain.

If you have a limited relationship with someone, especially any relationship that has a lot of illusions in it, they can't 'leave leave' because there isn't a real relationship to leave and there's no real commitment. Much of the pain that ensues is actually about how when they leave (or you feel like they are or are going to) any illusions that you had about them have to leave also and you resist stepping into reality.

If you're limited in your capacity to love and choosing limited experiences and limited people to make a limited contribution with, you're never getting that close that it will hurt to the fullest extent of your fears, because you never really believed they were going to stay anyway. If you never really believed someone would stay or that you could hold onto them, you wouldn't give yourself to the fullest even if you convinced yourself you were. You wouldn't. It might feel like a lot of effort that you're putting out there, but this is the case for all unavailable people – due to the way you handle yourself emotionally and your love habits, it's bound to feel like you're climbing Mount Everest when, at times, with some of the people you're engaging with it's more like climbing a molehill.

When you have a squeeze on your emotional capacity, it's like trying to run with a weight around your ankle or your hands tied to your sides – you'll move, it'll just take a lot of effort regardless of whether you're

going one metre or a hundred.

Unless you address your fear of abandonment you will either live in fear that they're going to leave killing the relationship with insecurity anyway, choose people that are likely to leave and end up acting in sync with the drama with it ending in them leaving, or sabotage relationships that don't look like they're going to meet your prophecy. This means that as long as you have a fear of abandonment, you're always going to be experiencing it, not least because you keep abandoning yourself in the process.

When you stop fearing abandonment, you can no longer be abandoned, not least because you will change how you view it and stop giving away all of your power.

And here's the thing: As children, we have very little control over our lives, if any at all, and so being deserted is abandonment because we are unable to take care of ourselves. We need to be nurtured, cared for, loved, respected and raised, and sometimes our parents don't do a very good job of this. There's also abandonment as in literally being deserted and then there is also having a sense of being abandoned because, in spite of the fact that our parent was 'there', they weren't there for you and you may have been left to fend for yourself emotionally and physically, or bad things happened and they didn't meet your expectations.

We rightly have an expectation that our parents should be there for us, but the reality is that this is not always the case, or that when they are, it's not always as we had envisioned it would be. It's not because something is fundamentally wrong with you – it's about their own flaws and failings. I talk about this more in *Mr Unavailable and The Fallback Girl*, but ultimately our parents aren't and weren't infallible and they do fail to meet our expectations at times, or even always. It is horrible to be abandoned, but it's a reflection of their actions, not your worth as a person. As a child it is easy to see how we can make the link between seemingly not being good enough and parents disappointing or even abandoning, but, as adults, it's time to change that association.

You arrived into this world good enough and you are always good enough – you just evolve over time. As an adult, you are now responsible for you. Even if you were in a relationship, you'd still be responsible for you, and ultimately, you are behind the wheel of your life and have control, so there is a limited amount of genuine abandonment you can experience in life if you're not only in reality, but you don't resign your value, hopes and life over to external influences.

Ironically, the chief abandoner in your life is actually you – you've deserted reality and you also keep deserting yourself in the pursuit of 'love'. Let me assure you – there are no prizes for this, so you can immediately claw back some sense of self by coming back to earth and discovering the real you that you already are, who's getting distracted in all of these fantasy escapades.

It's also important to note that breakups, lack of interest and dates not progressing isn't abandonment. It will look like this when you feel that you're being tossed back out to a life you don't want and a person (you) that you don't want. When you change how you feel about you and stop walking around with a person-shaped hole looking for validation and to be created and defined by others, you don't have to fear desertion because you have you when you go into a relationship, you still remain you and have you during it, and you can continue to be you and be there for you afterwards. It doesn't mean that if a relationship ends that you won't feel hurt, but it certainly won't be about feeling like your whole identity and world has walked off.

STUCK IN A PATTERN OF COPING

& RELATING

All the avoidance in your life has caused you to remain stuck in old patterns because of learned mechanisms of coping and relating that you find hard to let go of. They're how you feel you survive, it's just unfortunately with your survival kit being primarily made up of avoidance gear, you don't thrive; you tread water in the peripheries of your own life and others'. In fact, depending on how much fantasising you do, you may actually be standing outside of your own life and have retreated to your unconscious.

The ways in which you choose to relate to others is all linked in to your fear of rejection, the intimacy avoidance, the dodging responsibility, the sensitivity to conflict and criticism and trying to protect yourself from being abandoned. Unfortunately, you're so busy trying to cater to and manage all of these concerns, that you end up relating inwardly. It may feel like you're relating with others, but what you say and do is overshadowed by your tumultuous relationship with yourself and previous experiences that influence your behaviour and thinking in the first place.

Like all people in unavailable relationships, you give out with a view to what you're going to get back. It's not necessarily a conscious thing, but what you think others should be, do and give, normally equates to what you're missing from yourself and would ultimately like to get back. This can be in direct contradiction with the other person's agenda or capabilities.

Because you're so inwardly focused, it also means you're not always really listening, communicating, or engaging because your mind is already racing off, making assumptions, stirring up your inner critic, and adjusting your actions and what you say. It's all about being 'good enough', not being hurt, avoiding, 'winning' and being in with a chance – the way you operate in your relationships is your style of coping and relating.

You've figured out that going inward has buffered you against the pains of the world.

Fantasising is a great escape – your life can be better than what it is right now. Opting out of reality and imagining yourself in better situations, and feeling and being all that you'd like to be, can often help you cope with distancing yourself from very painful situations in real life. As a child, you can fantasise that your 'real' mother is going to show up one day and whisk you off to a wonderful life, or that you'll stumble across a secret letter that confirms that you're adopted, or that you have friends and loving people who understand what you're going through and protect you from the evils of the world.

Fantasy helps you to stop feeling alone and can give you the illusion of being loved and cared for and this can be enough to get you through your life, especially if in your vision, you never have to deal with anything uncomfortable or unpleasant, and you're getting all your hopes and expectations met.

You can escape your conscious thoughts and feelings, including avoiding simmering anger, frustration, or blame you've been piling on yourself, or even depression. It's a break and a distraction because I can tell you from personal experience that it can get exhausting and debilitating to listen to you mentally running yourself down, or feeling bad, or trying to deal with problems in the real world.

You don't want to be sad all the time. You don't want to have to pay attention to the I'm Not Good Enough backing track that's playing in your life.

The thing about coping is that it will only get you so far if your way of coping is not to address an issue, to overcome it, to confront your fears and feelings, to take your power and manage it, but to do just enough to scrape by and take the edge off or numb the pain. The problems will still be there – you're just distanced from them or are silencing yourself. It's also safe to say that it's not even the beginning of being an effective means of dealing with something, if your solution is to strip yourself of love, care, trust, and respect in real life.

The way to cope with someone else's inability to love you is not to tell yourself that it's because you're unlovable, no more than it is to tell yourself that you deserved abuse, or that there must be 'good' reasons for why bad things have happened to you while at the same time loathing yourself for buying into these ideas.

You've made so many judgements about yourself, love, and relationships based on your various experiences that your coping and relating is actually code for catering to a self-fulfilling prophecy, which of course ends up confirming the worst. This isn't because the things that you believe are absolutely true, but they are 'true' in the context of doing and experiencing certain things and making negative associations about them due to your beliefs.

If you believe you're not good enough and, that in order to feel good enough, you have to get external validation from a reluctant or outright unwilling source, then when you don't get it, it will confirm your belief that you're not good enough.

But if you were someone who treated yourself with love, care, trust and respect and decided you were good enough, aside from validating yourself, when someone isn't interested or unable to love you, you wouldn't believe that someone else's actions and inabilities had anything to do with your worth as a person. That's two different outlooks in the same situation taking away something different.

I'm a firm believer that when something is positively working for you, please keep on and knock yourself out doing it. While you may be 'coping' by sticking to a tried and tested route of carrying the same baggage, beliefs and behaviours and gravitating to variations of your type and similar situations, this isn't working for you.

Your pattern isn't working for you. You are not going to find love, care, trust, and respect in an uncomfortable comfort zone where you're subsisting on crumbs.

It works in that you're in your comfort zone, but the results of your actions and choices are reflected in your life, one, I might add, you're not that crazy about. The fact that you keep trying to do the same things and have the same mentality but you persist in trying to get a different result, shows that this isn't working for you.

The answer is not to try even harder to avoid all of the things that you don't like – you'll be on another planet at this rate! Stubbornness is refusal to change your course of action in spite of compelling reasons to do so and insanity is doing the same thing and expecting a different result – if you want a different result, you've got to start living a different life, not just coping with the current habits that aren't working for you.

CONTROLLING YOUR

EXPERIENCES

In your head and with the self-fulfilling prophecy, you can decide what happens and be in control of what you do and don't do. This means that sometimes when you appear to be having a burst of confidence and taking a 'risk', you're actually quietly punishing yourself and reminding you of all of your unhealthy beliefs about yourself, love and relationships. Bearing in mind that you have a self-fulfilling prophecy and these beliefs that you act in accordance with, when you 'dabble' with dating and relationships, it can be a bit like when someone gets exasperated with being told that they can or 'should' do something, so grudgingly and resentfully, they do it, often half-heartedly and even sabotaging themselves along the way, and then go, 'See! I told you it doesn't work!'

I've seen this happen a few times with people who have lost their confidence about their professional capabilities. An interview is arranged for them by someone who does believe in them, or after they've half-heartedly applied for a job and surprised themselves by landing an interview, and then they show up late, or badly dressed, or they answer questions but don't really make an effort and exude an air of being there not by choice, but by force. Of course they don't get the job and even though they really did not put 100% into going for the role, they get all righteous and aggrieved about not getting the job and having tried.

After Yet Another Dubious Dating Experience, you can say, 'I knew he was a bastard and I was right not to want to put myself out there,' but the thing is, bastard or not, you neglect to acknowledge that you weren't putting yourself out there anyway, so you're actually linking two things together that exist independently of each other, not because of each other. It's the same when you say, 'I knew he was too good to be true and that I was better off not dating.' That's bullshit, because if you thought it was too good to be true, you didn't have to believe and you could have left instead of going along with the facade. It's also not that you're better off not dating – what you're better off doing is not continuing to be with people who you know are talking out of their arse and instead forging your interactions in reality. It also might help if you showed up with a modicum of trust because, if you don't trust anyway, it wouldn't matter if you were going out with The Most Trustworthy Person On The Planet™, you'd still be wondering where the catch was.

- If you don't go out, you get to control how much interaction and risk you experience.

- If you keep going out with the same type of person that generates the same dodgy result, while you may complain, you're actually controlling how much you try and limiting the amount of hurt and risk you experience.

- If you go out with people who confirm your unhealthy and unrealistic beliefs, which in turn you use to compound judgements that you've made about yourself, you also get to control the unhealthy perception of you.

- If you keep involving yourself in situations that confirm your unhealthy and unrealistic beliefs, you also get to control the opportunity to change.

- If you don't allow you to experience true intimacy and commitment, you control how much of your emotions you have to access and limit the amount of risk you expose yourself to.

- If you spend most of your time in your head, that's easier to control than external forces beyond your control.

You might believe that you're putting yourself out there because, contextually, it may be a huge effort for you, or slightly more than the last time, but, contextually, as in with real life and the effort that's needed for a relationship, you're not trying. You're not. I say this from experience – there's no easier way to remain in your comfort zone, or even feel sorry for yourself and convinced of your lack of options, than to continue rationalising thoughts and behaviour that you know are not working for you so that you can continue lying to yourself.

You're able to control your experiences because you are habitually being dishonest with yourself and you use 'feedback' from life and your private ruminations to construct an argument to remain in your comfort zone. What you forget though is that just because you think or feel something, it doesn't make it fact, plus when you continue to try to forge unhealthy relationships, you're using unhealthy thinking to try to control the uncontrollable, i.e. the people that you're involved with.

You'll discover that when you force yourself to be real and address your beliefs, those arguments tumble like a house of cards, especially as it actually requires a lot more effort and creates a lot more pain to continue lying and basing subsequent actions in a real relationship off the back of it, than it does to accept reality. What you've also discovered from your experiences is that having an illusion of control is not the same as actually having control, and that it would be better to take control positively of yourself, than to continue trying to control your experiences so that you can hold onto negative beliefs that help you to create a negative life.

Moving Forward

IT'S TIME TO WAKE UP & LIVE

Real relationships require vulnerability. You have to take a certain amount of risk, engage, get to know someone, share yourself, put yourself out there, experience, address and resolve conflict, love, care, trust, respect and put both of your feet into them so that you're not metaphorically halfway out the door with your bags packed waiting for it to fuck up. You've got to be in and do all of these things and more, and the reality, is that, yes, there's a possibility that it might not work out. In fact, you might get hurt or hurt them, make mistakes, not always act in ways that are conducive to healthy relationships, not always agree, get angry, be fearful, express your fears, make ill judgements, or have circumstances come out of left field that change, challenge and even break the relationship.

This is all a part of life. To fear these things is to fear living.
To withdraw into a fantasy is to opt out of living, although I hate to break it to you, but your life is proceeding anyway, it's just by treating your body like some empty shell going through the motions of life, you're doing yourself a disservice.
To fear being vulnerable is to shut down.
To try to limit the risk and in fact live a life of no 'new pain', and no 'new vulnerability' and no 'new risk' is to take shelter in relationships that have you on a diet of crumbs and will actually leave you feeling emotionally, physically and spiritually neglected.

You cannot reach your full potential through fantasy.

Unhealthy relationships are like living on a diet of crumbs and fantasy

---

143

relationships will leave you hungry and malnourished. The dissatisfaction you'll feel, along with the disparity between reality and your imagination, will actually leave you hungry for something more 'real life'. Just like the fantasy isn't real, neither is the illusion that your life is perfect, safe, full, joyous, rewarding etc. It's not. It's not. It's time to move beyond what you've been experiencing and nourish you so that you can fill up your life with real experiences.

Over the following chapters, I've shared tips, tools and inspiration for breaking your dreamer habit and overcoming your fears. Coupled with *Mr Unavailable and The Fallback Girl* which has a detailed guide on taking the steps to becoming available plus any additional support you seek to help you on your journey, you can exert power you already possess within you to make real, positive change in your life.

TAKING A DIFFERENT VIEW ON

'REJECTION'

I was watching *Homeland* recently, a Showtime series featuring Claire Danes as a CIA agent who doesn't believe a prisoner of war's story after he returns to America. She believes that he has been turned and is working for Al Qaeda. Her primary fear is avoiding another 9/11, for which she blames herself for missing something. Her boss tells her, 'Everyone missed something that day.' This is completely true and it boggles the mind that one person would assume the blame for a situation where there was more than one cog in the wheel, and it's the same for your relationships – if all you focus on is your element and bear the brunt of all of the blame, then make a judgement about you and change your behaviour and sense of self off the back of it, it's a distorted view and a subsequently rather distorted mission.

You don't equal the relationship.

Yes, it's very possible that when an ex has ended things or not turned out to be who you thought they were, that you experienced conflict over your incompatibilities, but, ultimately, the end of a relationship or dates not blossoming into one, represents the breaking of the 'relationship deal' or turning down the perceived deal on offer.

Relationships take two, not one. When someone opts out or chooses not

to proceed, they're turning down their part in it too.

Let me say it again: you don't equal the relationship, so the relationship ending or not happening cannot directly correlate to your worth as a person. If you do correlate it to your worth, you're saying that what has or hasn't come to be rests wholly and solely on you, i.e. you equal the relationship. This begs the question though: If you make a relationship ending or not materialising into a reflection of you as a person, where does it leave the other party? Why isn't their worth affected?

By being focused on what you perceive as a rejection of you, you're assuming that you did something 'wrong' – you're giving away all your power in that moment. What if they don't have the emotional capacity and ability to give you what you want? That's about them, not you. What about if they're not over their ex? You could be The Most Amazing Person That Ever Graced This Earth™, but their emotions are still tied up elsewhere. What if they're not ready to sign up to a 'deal'? Yep, still not you – their readiness is about *their* readiness.

Of course, you may argue that if you were being and doing certain things (basically you were 'good enough'), then they'd feel ready, but this is to imply that readiness is not something that's in possession of our being and is down to an external party to create, when there are plenty of people out there serving as evidence of being involved with 'ready' people, but losing them because they weren't ready. That, and making it about you is to suggest that there are no other issues in existence – this just flat out isn't true. They may have mitigating circumstances – personal problems. They're 'personal' for a reason. You might feel like love conquers all, but they don't. That's not rejection – that's them needing to handle their own business so that they can truly develop the capacity for a healthy relationship, even if, in the end, it's not with you.

Rejection is feeling that you've not been shown due care (hence you feel uncared for), or being turned down, which leaves you feeling that you weren't up to 'standard'. It has many negative connotations attached to it because it's tied to notions of being 'sub-par', inadequate, failing, rebuffed, declined, refused, abandoned, deserted, brushed off, inappropriate and, ultimately, not good enough.

In dating and relationships, 'rejection' in the sense of being chosen to proceed with, is impossible to avoid, because not all dates and relationships are supposed to work out – that's why dating is a discovery phase – and even if it progresses into a relationship, it might not work. Short of only ever being with one person, you will have to turn people down, let go, and break up with them and vice versa. That's why there are single people and breakups.

Not being chosen by every date and the possibility of a relationship not working out is unavoidable and being able to say NO, to opt out of situations, to admit when something isn't working, is all part of the natural order of freeing yourself up to be available for a mutual relationship.

Acceptance of reality sometimes means walking away from something good when you know that you want something different to them, or don't actually have anything to match – this is why many relationships end, it's just that we often don't recognise the blessing in disguise as we're too busy nursing the 'wound' and our ego's. You don't equal the relationship and you don't equal the world either, so when you stop seeing what others do and the world at large as being a reflection of your worth and separate them into individual entities with their own agenda, it takes a weight of rejection off.

QUIT THE REJECTION LINGO

We all experience rejection, but you'll notice that those who cope with and move on from rejection, don't call it 'rejection' – they call it 'breaking up', 'not working out', 'not getting the job', 'the friendship growing apart', 'different priorities', 'wanting different things', a 'disagreement', 'they said NO' etc. What they don't do is make what equates to semi-permanent and permanent judgements about themselves off the back of these experiences.

They don't nurse the breakup for long periods of time and deem themselves not up to standard for any other relationship or life itself.

They don't blame themselves for why the relationship didn't work out.

They don't decide never to interview for another job, abandon their passion and disregard their hopes and plans.

Even though they'll be hurt, they recognise some of the contributing factors as to why the friendship changed.

They accept that they weren't in agreement about what each regarded as very important.

They recognise that on the things that mattered, they didn't have shared values.

They accept that conflict can and will happen and that it has nothing to do with their worthiness and everything to do with a difference of opinion, a dispute, incompatibility on an area, or even a misunderstanding.

They accept that they can't hear YES all the time, just like they can't give a YES all the time either.

It's critical that you recognise that only people who have already internalised rejection and made a judgement about themselves, talk and think about dating, relationships or even life in terms of 'rejection'. These are the people who have low, or even no self-esteem and who partake in unhealthy relationships.

Using rejection lingo to talk and think about situations is indicative of these experiences being used as a way of gaining acceptance through validation, or that certainly post fallout, you now perceive them as a 'lost opportunity' for acceptance.

By hanging onto the rejection and speaking the lingo, you're sending that rejection snowball downhill and causing it to grow in relative importance to your life. What you fail to register is that the size and impact of the rejection is wholly down to you – it doesn't have to be this big. You could have chucked the snowball away and splatted it with your self-esteem or reality.

If you didn't internalise these experiences and change how you feel about you, it's not that you wouldn't be upset by a relationship not working out, but that's what you would be upset over, not this idea that you didn't measure up, that you've 'failed' as a person, and that ultimately you're not 'good enough' and acceptable and accepted.

Moving forward, you have to make a critical, conscious effort to adjust your mental and verbal relationship vocabulary, which will stop you seeing life through a rejection lens where everything is about your lack of 'worthiness'. You're putting way too much of you into the events of the world and the actions of those around you – people are too caught up in themselves, doing their own thing for their own agenda, to surrender themselves to you and suddenly change their personality and their motivations off the back of what they perceive you to be. How worthy we are is down to us. There are people out there who appear to have 'everything' who still don't think and feel that they're worthy – it is you that needs to change your view of you.

No more of this 'I can't handle rejection', or 'I can't bear the thought of having to deal with another date not working out', or 'There has to be something seriously wrong with me', or 'I wish I'd rejected them first before they did it to me', or 'Them moving on makes me feel even more rejected', or 'I must have done something to cause all of this.'

STOP. Every time you think or say something that sounds like rejection talk, halt yourself and rephrase. This stops your mind and mouth from running away from you, but it also forces you to make a conscious effort to be in reality.

Where you're saying 'I' a lot and taking on blame, it's time to start using 'we' and also balancing with 'they'. It's bad enough that you'd sit around thinking and chatting shit about yourself, but at least have the brass neck to call a spade a spade with them. If you can find it in you to be compassionate about them, you need to turn that energy towards you also.

'I should have tried harder' is actually: 'We should have tried harder.'

'I feel like my neediness pushed them away' is actually: 'I do feel like my neediness may have pushed them away, but, at the same time, it's important to remember that they said X or did Y and Z happened. While I could stand to manage my insecurities which I'm going to address before I start a new relationship, they're not the reason why the relationship ended. It's a mixture of factors from both of us – even if I had myself together, that wouldn't have changed who they were.'

Rejection talk is a means of lying to yourself.

This isn't about pretending that incidences of rejection don't exist but, it is about recognising that blaming you and obsessing over what you think are the reasons why you haven't been 'chosen', keep you stuck in a fantasy where you avoid everything uncomfortable, or a fantasy where you use these lies to persecute yourself, or a fantasy that you use to form the basis of your next mission. As you're being unrealistic in general, never mind about yourself, using what you believe are reasons for you being 'rejected' to drive your decisions, means that you never learn and grow out of any of your experiences, and in fact repeat your habits in yet another unhealthy liaison. Changing how you speak about these experiences and ultimately how you think about yourself, will dramatically reduce your self-blame.

DON'T USE 'REJECTION' TO MAKE JUDGEMENTS ABOUT YOU – OVERTURN YOUR WRONGFUL CONVICTION

You dating or being in a relationship is not about convincing the other party not to reject you. If this is your directive and you fundamentally don't feel good enough off your own steam, these are not dates or relationships; they're Mission Impossibles.

When you devote so much of your energy to thinking about things in terms of rejection and being good enough for them not to reject you, where are you evaluating your interest in them? Or, are you only interested in what they can do for you – accept you, fill you up, make you whole, make your life good and complete?

Why is this person more powerful than you?
Why does this person have the 'expertise' to accept you? What are their qualifications?
Why are you to blame if things don't proceed or work out?
Why are you making yourself responsible for whether the relationship succeeds?
Why do you have to have 'done' or 'been' something for this so-called 'rejection' to happen?
Why can't you experience NO in life?

Change how you feel about and cope with rejection by avoiding using it as a something to make a judgement about yourself on. Judge the situation first with the both of you in it, before you even think about making it all about you.

It's also about time you found some new descriptors and labels – your default setting can't be 'I'm not good enough'. There are a million reasons why things happen in this world – you can stand to find at least ten that don't involve you making what ultimately leads back to a judgement about you that deems you 'not good enough'. When you've found your first ten, find another ten, then another, then another.

Desperation, convincing, seeking validation, wearing your insecurity like a coat with flashing neon messaging on it and giving people the responsibility to determine your worth and make your life ain't sexy or attractive.

Part of being a grown-up is that we have to stop throwing all our toys out of the pram when things don't go our way, and let go of that naivety we may have held onto since we were children where we're still thinking and acting like everything that comes out of our parents' mouths is correct, every action is 'right', and so, in turn, anyone and anything similar to them, is confirming their rightness.

There is an assumption that if a parent or caretaker has done something (or failed to be something), that it's a reflection on us as a child. This means you may have made a judgement about yourself long ago based on distorted and false evidence seen through a child's eyes. It's like a wrongful conviction, only you've been punishing you for it ever since. As you're the judge, you're actually the person who has the power to let it go and stand corrected. It's time for you to overturn that conviction.

USE PERSPECTIVE TO LESSEN THE IMPACT OF REJECTION IN YOUR LIFE

Certainly for your romantic relationships, you can ease some of the sting of rejection by evaluating the pressures that you're using for your rejection 'metrics'. Having your own aspirations, desires and goals is fine, but they're actually separate to your dating and relationship experiences. When you take rejection hard, you're making some dangerous assumptions that tie your metrics to unrelated external factors.

You have your own agenda as does everyone else and ultimately will find a greater level of happiness with someone who has a similar

That said, when dates or relationships haven't worked out, it's not like they've been evaluating whether you should meet your aspirations, desires and goals – they have their own. To assume otherwise, is to treat it like, 'This date didn't work out. I'm obviously not good enough to have a relationship/get married or have children one day.'

Now, while you have a pattern to your relationship experiences, don't just throw them all into the relationship pot like a big fat rejection – they are all different, unique experiences, that, while they may share commonalities, have different feedback and lessons to take on board.

They may all look the same because you tell yourself the same message afterwards – that you're not good enough, you've been rejected, you've failed, you're not up to standard etc – but they are not the same and it will serve you well to distinguish between them as it will help you to not only deal with each experience, but to cut to the heart of the original rejection and overcome it.

IDENTIFY YOUR REJECTION BEHAVIOUR

What do you do that demonstrates your fear of rejection? The easiest way to way to see your behaviour is to identify someone from whom you fear rejection.

What do you do to avoid it? Write down a list of specific behaviours and actions that you engage in. E.g. 'I back down quickly', 'I have sex with them quickly as I'm afraid to say NO in case they lose interest', 'I don't question anything', 'I get increasingly sexually risque to hold them.'

At the time when you do these things, are you responding to something

that's actually happening or something you fear might happen? Going through your list will tell you if you were doing stuff to respond to anxiety within or whether you were responding to specific things that were happening in a relationship that wasn't working that you panicked about experiencing rejection from. This will tell you whether you need to address anxiety or boundaries and other relationship habits.

What do you think that each act will achieve? Divide them into short-, medium- and long-term aims.

Looking at each one, have any of them produced the desired medium- to long-term result? Ultimately, when all is said and done, did you after undertaking all of these endeavours, manage to avoid rejection?

Repeat these questions for all of your significant relationships. If you haven't had any significant relationships (in love, together for several months or years, heartbroken), then look at your dates. Assessing your dates against the questions above immediately gives you a sense of your dating habits and what type of instant gratification and short-term behaviour you engage in.

What you can immediately learn from identifying your rejection avoidance behaviour and your pattern, is where you need to change. You are not experiencing the desired outcome and none of these things leave you feeling good about you.

Go through the list and identify how you really feel after each item. For example, 'I back down quickly....and then I feel silenced and like I've let myself down', or 'I have sex with them quickly as I'm afraid to say NO in case they lose interest... and then I feel empty and devalued plus they end up losing interest anyway.' And, by the way, they don't lose interest because of your worth; if there's a direct or indirect pressure to have sex, they were unlikely to be sticking around anyway. What you discover is the contrast between what you intended to achieve and what actually happened, which just goes to show that this behaviour isn't working for you.

Is any of the behaviour that you engage in similar to that with a parent? If yes, work through the questions above with each parent. What you immediately learn here is where you have adopted a pattern of coping and relating from childhood that hasn't evolved and matured into adulthood. You may also be picking similar people to your parents, which is like trying to right the wrongs of the past. If in doubt, make a list of the positive and negative qualities and characteristics of your parents and the people you identified above and cross check for similarities.

If it's not your parents/carer, can you identify the specific relationship or situation that triggered a change in your behaviour and has you catering to your fear of rejection? This is the critical rejection experience that needs to be addressed as it's the unresolved feelings, the impact of the stress and, ultimately, the judgement that you have made about yourself and subsequent changes to your behaviour and thinking that's sent you down a path of engaging in your relationships in this manner.

What happened? List 5-10 key things that happened (you can of course do more but prioritising will certainly also help you to see the top line data of what went wrong) that caused this to be a particularly painful rejection that you haven't recovered from.

For each thing that happened, what is the specific judgement you made about yourself as a consequence? What conclusion did you draw about you? If you thought you were something before this incident and decided that you weren't after, what was it?

Of what you've listed, what are you taking all or most of the blame for? Of the things that you've blamed you and made a judgement about you that fuels you adapting your behaviour to avoid rejection, which of these are you 100% responsible for and which had at least one other party involved in it?

Of the reasons that you've listed, are they the actual reasons about why the relationship broke down? Or are they reasons that you've latched onto that have formed the basis of your blame cycle? It is critical that you take another look at the list and ask, 'Why did we break up?' or 'What really happened here?'

- Were there any code amber or red issues in the relationship? If there were, are they listed and if not, why not? There's a list of code amber and red behaviour in *Mr Unavailable and the Fallback Girl* but you're basically looking to identify anything that crosses boundaries by causing discomfort and that flags unhealthy behaviour and situations. This includes anything that has previously caused you pain and/or represents where you may be repeating a pattern from childhood including choosing partners with similar issues to one or both parents.

- Was there a difference in core values that would have rendered you incompatible regardless of anything that you did or didn't do? If there were, are they listed and if not, why not?

- Does the list include the behaviour of the other party or at least things that you both contributed to? If the list only has what you've done, you are lying to yourself and assuming the blame for everything which makes you responsible for 'everything' without you actually being genuinely accountable and responsible for your part.

- Were there any concerns that you overrode? If there were, are they listed and if not, why not?

What you can immediately see from the list is what the real issues are and where you may be stubbornly holding onto blame when you could be seeing the bigger, more realistic picture that would actually leave you less rejected.

Is there a relationship (romantic or otherwise) where you didn't/don't have the fear of being rejected? If yes, why? This will give you a sense of what factors contribute to you feeling confident about your worth – are they internal – how you positively feel about you? Or external – how you perceive others to feel about you or how good your life is?

- What did/do you feel around them?
- What were/are they doing?
- If this is a relationship you're no longer involved in, what was your life like at that point in time? For example, were you happy at work? Friendships good? Family interaction positive? Hobbies and interests? Happy within yourself? Less breakups under your belt?

Has your life changed greatly since that point in time and, if so, why? Identify specific things that have altered the satisfaction with your life. e.g. Redundancy, not recovering from a painful loss, a fall out with a family member, health concerns, abandoning the things you cared about for one particular relationship and not getting back on track afterwards. What could you do to reintroduce the positive elements into your life?

Can you identify a specific reason why you felt confident about not being rejected? Or, looking at it from another perspective, what made you feel accepted in this relationship? Some people, for instance, feel confident about not being rejected because they feel like they have all of the power in the relationship and that the person has them on a pedestal.
If this is a relationship you're no longer involved in, why did it end?

Did you experience any feelings of rejection after you left the relationship where you had felt confident? If yes, why? If you had regrets about certain things or blamed yourself for why the relationship ended, what were they and now, with the benefit of hindsight, can you be more realistic about the situation?

Use the rejection avoidance behaviours and patterns that you've identified as a springboard for addressing your fears of rejection and where you need to adapt your behaviour. You can see specifically what you are doing and the lack of results it generates and ultimately the negative impact on you – it leaves you feeling rejected because it's self-rejection anyway. You can then identify where you need to be more assertive, to set boundaries, to be more patient before you're so quick to compromise or silence yourself, and where you could do with some more self-control, such as with sexual activities. All rejection avoidance behaviour needs to gradually change – they are habits, that even though they may be long held, they can be broken because they don't serve you.

REJECTION – A BLESSING IN DISGUISE

Rejection paves the way to opening a new door in your life. While it can and often does hurt, them doing what you may not be able to do for yourself frees you up to gain perspective and be available for yourself and a more fulfilling relationship... if you don't avoid it.

If you were actually in something that detracted from you and had a load of code amber (stop, look and listen concerns and don't proceed until addressed) and red (halt and stop painting red flags green warnings), them 'turning you down' is actually a blessing in disguise. Let them skip on down the street and find someone else to mess with.

Stop feeling bad about the fact that someone who you knew (whether you choose to admit it or not) had clear signs that they weren't capable of being the person you wanted them to be or giving you the relationship you want, didn't 'change' for you.

The funny thing is – you not accepting someone is... rejection. You're feeling rejected about the fact that they didn't change from what you find rejectionable.

You don't have to see rejection as something terrible.

The relationships that have formed part of the experiences that have made you rejection shy – you were in these relationships too. Instead of rejecting the truth of who they are or the experiences, accept them and recognise that you're 'out' for a damn good reason!

People are allowed to say NO to you. They are. Don't panic though – it cuts both ways!

Equally, if you're feeling rejected because your hopes for a person and a relationship that fuelled a fantasy haven't come to fruition, the sense of rejection will ease when you bring your hopes back down to earth and grieve them. The hopes you had were real, but they were your hopes so if you want to feel less rejected (and I imagine you do), reality check those hopes and recognise that they can't reject your hopes – they're yours.

You can't just wallow in pain or stick to a relationship/fantasy that detracts from you like glue just because it's better than feeling 'rejection rejection'.
Some of the things you see as rejection aren't rejection – it's giving you an Early Opt Out with no penalties, a difference of opinion, or NO.
Them not changing = them not changing.
Different values = wanted different things.
Disagreement = disagreement.
They couldn't give you what you want (even if they talked out of their bum and claimed that they could) = overestimated capacity and Betting On Potential.

Even if they were 'great', they're just not that special that you should deem yourself some sort of 'rejection case'. You wanted different things – that sounds a hell of a lot better than 'They rejected me', especially because rejection automatically creates the assumption that you are wholly and solely responsible for why the relationship hasn't worked out or why they behave as they do – you're not.

Don't see your relationships as a 'waste' or that you are now 'rejectionable' – that's writing off both bad and good times. Not all relationships can or are meant to last and to wallow in rejection or to avoid it, is to also disregard the truth.

Maybe there are things you could have done differently but guess what? You weren't alone. Whatever your relationship was supposed to be, it's been, even if you would have preferred it to be something different. Instead of feeling crap about everything you didn't get that you think you were entitled to – remember who they were and why it's over. If there's some good in there, great, but if what you're mourning is the loss of what didn't happen, don't 'waste' your life by devoting it to taking up pain and rejection solitude as a vocation.

Same goes for dates – dating is a discovery phase! Trust me when I say you haven't discovered anything so fabulous about a date that warrants you carrying on like they were the last chance saloon!

You wanted different things. You had a difference of opinion. They're not ready for commitment whether it's you in the hot seat or The Most Perfect Person in the Universe. Whatever it is – it's not the definition of you.

LEARN TO MANAGE YOUR

DISAPPOINTMENT

Don't pretend that you're not disappointed – aside from invalidating how you really feel, the truth is that even with something brief, we have hopes that need to be let go of. Giving yourself the space to work through the loss is a much more self-nurturing approach than festering in disappointment – it helps you to gain perspective, that thing that if it's missing, turns disappointment into rejection.

Have you got carried away?
Do they know you in full to truly have rejected you?
Where does the disappointment stem from?
Are there other reasons that don't put it all on you for the reason for the disappointment?

Take a broader view – don't make it all about you.

Will turning the disappointment inward cause you to stray from who you are – your values? Don't try to be a goody two shoes – pretending to be nice and avoiding judgement of the situation or even their actions, leads to unexpressed anger and frustration, which can if allowed to continue, turn to depression if you turn all of this negativity inwards. While most won't admit it, trying to be 'good' is a way of taking the higher road that leaves you not only at the mercy of being a doormat, but on a pedestal that suggests that you're better than being a normal person that gets angry, when you actually do.

Where does what happened and what you hoped it might become, fit in with your plans? Was the reality different from your values? When disappointment envelops you and gets out of hand, it's refusal to accept – this will become a sting of rejection.

But is it disappointment? Or is it rejection?

`Disappointment` is the feeling of displeasure and sadness caused by the non-fulfilment of your hopes and expectations – this isn't the same as rejection. You can be disappointed without rejection having a damn thing to do with it – you are blanket labelling the feeling of disappointment and jumping straight to rejection. You've likely experienced a lot of disappointment, but less rejection than you actually think you have.

Disappointment, like conflict, fear and even rejection is unavoidable. The power and the growth though, lies in how you handle it and move beyond. There's no point in devoting your energy to avoiding disappointment – it happens all the time.

Disappointment becomes rejection when you experience unhappiness over your hopes and expectations not being fulfilled and you in turn make a judgement about you. You can't afford to make a judgement about you every time things don't go your way – things don't go everybody's way a lot.

Disappointment lifts with self-care and perspective – it can feel like you have clouds over you when you experience it, but what you have to remember is that the clouds will pass and that there is sky there. What you don't want to do is become so buried in the disappointment that it becomes all that you can see.

It's very difficult to have perspective or take care of yourself if your default mode is to blame yourself and/or to let your life be derailed.

By not practising acceptance, you can become disproportionately invested – in the cold light of day when your ego calms down and you gain perspective, it can be disconcerting to discover that what you feel disappointment for might not even be something that you want.

Don't allow disappointment to eat up you and your life. If you neglect or even abuse yourself when you experience disappointment, it compounds it and turns it into rejection and makes it that much harder to recover from.

If disappointment has been a mainstay of your life recently or even over a significant period of time, your hopes and expectations not being fulfilled has turned into rejection and in turn, you've made a judgement about you as a result. Over the years of writing Baggage Reclaim, I've found that among the toughest struggles is letting go of the hopes and, yes, sometimes the illusions that you had for a person and a relationship with them. There can be sustained periods of rumination and in essence, stewing in what you feel is a rejection of you, and if there have been a series of disappointments, you have likely lost you along the way. In losing sight of your values, you don't have the perspective that's so needed to be able to handle and manage the inevitable disappointments that arise in life.

When you struggle to recover from disappointment after a date doesn't materialise with someone you'd hoped for, or a number of dates and even a sexual involvement don't proceed into a relationship, or the person and the relationship you had with them doesn't work out plus they don't seem to be who you thought they were, all of your hopes and expectations are tied up in them.

You lose sight of the bigger picture. You lose your focus on your values, possibly because you may not be entirely aware of what your values are. Your hopes and expectations are tied to these values and when you become fixated on this person (or even a series of people that you thought were 'it' fulfilling your hopes and dreams, the disappointment can leave you feeling like there's no point in bothering and your 'last chance saloon' has gone.

The thing is, this person is not the only way that you could have your hopes and expectations for a relationship fulfilled plus just because they don't or didn't fulfil them, doesn't mean any and all hopes for a relationship are over.

When you struggle to get over the disappointment, it's because you were over-invested in the potential, 'vision', and ultimately the hopes, plans and outcome that you had set your mind and heart on.

If you were more big picture-orientated, which would root your perspective in your values and reality instead of the smoke and mirrors of what could, would, and should have been, you'd see that the 'dream' isn't over.

Your values and aspirations for happiness shouldn't all be tied in one person. They are not the only person you can have a relationship with – broaden your horizons. If you have been invested in various people and the hopes and expectations you had for a relationship have to adjust due to practical factors, the disappointment is natural and to be expected, but you have to work your way through these feelings to acceptance so that you can create new hopes and expectations. To continue to immerse yourself in disappointment like a vocation, will only leave you with regret, because as time passes and your outlook and what you're doing hasn't changed, that is what you'll come to regret – not the various things you've been through that brought you to this juncture but the stubbornness you used to lash yourself with a rejection and disappointment belt.

Holding onto disappointment will cause you to start to lose hope, which may lead to depression.

What do you want? This is where your focus should be – on the bigger picture of your values so that you can focus your actions on living congruently with them.

The disappointment, regret, and rejection is tied up in the idea that what you hope and want in your life is gone and over. Holding tight to this thought, it will only be natural to then rake over your past and ruminate on all of the things you 'coulda, woulda, shoulda' done if only which will perpetuate the regret, and pour more rejection on you.

Don't latch on to 'someone' and the hopes and illusions surrounding them, whether it's yours or theirs, to create your life for you – it's like waiting for someone to come and rescue you from your life and make it all better. If it doesn't work out, it's like returning to the life you didn't want in the first place.

Wherever there's disappointment and a sense of feeling rejected, you can be assured that there are illusions and they give you an inaccurate, if not downright distorted view of reality. It's letting go of these that give you much-needed perspective.

What are you stuck on? List them all, don't hold back. What is sticking in your craw about this disappointment that you keep returning to? You would not be disappointed if what you claim things 'should' be was real... because you'd be living it.

Walk your way through the relationship and work out where you got the illusions from.

- Where did it start?
- Did they say or do something? Did you?
- What did you think that led you to this idea?
- The things that you believed them to be, why did you believe it? Was it based on evidence? Was it brief? Was it based on beliefs that you carried into the relationship that may be based on someone else they remind you of?
- If you believe certain things about their qualities, characteristics etc, why and did they consistently demonstrate themselves to be this? List

examples and the longer you were together, the more you should see of this.

What is the cause of the actual disappointment? So, for example, when someone doesn't follow through with a date, is it because:

- You're disappointed because you misjudged them?
- They seemed so nice and you were looking forward to it?
- You hoped that this might be 'it' and you could be done with dating?
- You're disappointed because you assume that you must have said or done something to put them off?
- You compromised yourself and it still didn't pay off?
- You are shouldering all the blame for it not working out?
- You banked on this being the one that would make all of the previous heartache worthwhile and right the wrongs of the past?

Taking a bigger picture view, this person cannot meet your expectations. They haven't – it's why you're disappointed. They haven't – that's about them, not you.

If you make them not meeting your hopes and expectations solely about you, as if you performed Jedi mind tricks and 'made' them into something different, you lose perspective and again compound the loss and sense of rejection.

The facts say that they cannot meet your expectations – it's holding onto the illusions that they can or could have if only XYZ had happened, which normally boils down to, if you had changed, if you hadn't breathed or put a foot wrong, if you had got them to change, if you lived in a fantasy world, that's disappointing you.

Let me say it again – it's holding onto the illusions that they can or could have fulfilled your hopes and expectations and that your projected future could, would and should have happened that's disappointing you. The tighter you hold onto it, the more you revisit it, it's like experiencing the disappointment over and over and over again.

Disappointment and rejection paves the way to new and ultimately better opportunities… if you don't spend months or even years trying to avoid admitting a mistake or accepting that it's over. The longer you avoid is what turns the situation into a 'setback'.

One of the things that will release you to grow and let go is to make the connection between relationship insanity – carrying the same baggage, beliefs, and behaviours while choosing same type, different person (or variations of your type), and then expecting a different result – and disappointment.

Relationships serve to teach us about ourselves – the same lessons will keep coming back at you like Michael Myers in *Halloween* until you heed and learn from them.

If you persist in relationship insanity, you will continue to be disappointed. Even if you do the whole long-shot mentality thing and go with the safe option of unavailable relationships so you can avoid 'rejection rejection', you will be disappointed.

Your life and your repetitive choices are telling you that you need to adapt your thinking and your habits in order to start fulfilling your hopes and expectations for your life.

Your life and your repetitive choices are saying:

'[Insert your name], if you want to be loved, respected, trusted and cared for in a mutual relationship and be happy, this is not the way to go about it.

An unavailable person with their own agenda and thinking that may directly contradict what you have in mind, is already operating at a limited capacity and doesn't have sufficient capacity for medium to long-term commitment, and in some cases, even short-term. I know it's a pain in the arse and that it would be so much easier if you could take a shortcut and get someone who you think has similar fears and issues to you, to make you the exception to their rule of behaviour, but it's about time you made you the exception to your own rule of stubbornness. Stop fighting it and accept it.

When you do, you will realise that, yes, it's disappointing, but by heeding the message from this relationship and even your relationship 'resume', you are being helped towards your 'goal' of being in a loving, mutual relationship. These disappointments happened because they couldn't give you what you want. Yeah you could've been a doormat, silenced yourself, or downgraded your expectations, but you'd actually only be even more disappointed. Experience has already taught you this, so why continue down this road and hope to get a different result, when you could do something drastically different and live your life positively for an altogether different result?'

Accept what you can learn from this, even if some of those lessons are really uncomfortable like, 'Don't be a sucker for the hype, pay attention to contradicting actions and words, your private parts aren't a good judge of character, and stay off the relationship crack and keep your feet firmly in reality.'

Disappointment can be greatly lessened if you live in line with your values so that you can be authentic. If you stay on a Bullshit Diet, it also means that you don't hear what you want to hear, see what you want to see, and create meaning where there is none. You'll communicate your expectations, thoughts and concerns – some people don't do this for fear of disappointment. Then they get disappointed anyway and wish they'd spoken up. And maybe that's one of the greatest things you can learn about disappointment – you'll experience it but it won't hang around for long if you haven't got regret for the things you did to avoid disappointment and rejection that ultimately sold you short coupled with blame and shame. Don't try to be a perfectionist or the exception to the rule of shady behaviour – these create unrealistic goals while giving you a realistic but unwanted outcome: pain.

You don't have to let disappointment claim you and you certainly shouldn't use it to make judgements about yourself that leave you with eroded self-esteem. Let the disappointment go – holding onto the disappointment, ruminating over the coulda, woulda, shouldas, trying to get a retraction so you can avoid dealing with the disappointment, giving up your life, being disappointed in yourself, and festering in a pool of negativity, will only beget further disappointment. Forgive you and be kind to you because aside from nurturing you, it means you won't disappoint you by not being on your side.

FORGIVE YOU

When you realise how you've been treating yourself, it's easy to fall into the trap of self-blame and feeling like there's no hope. You may read this book, or others, hear advice, or see people endeavouring to make changes in their own lives, and feel like there's no hope for you due to 'all the things I've done to myself'. It would be easy now to look around and feel hopeless, to wonder where on earth you can start, to feel regret, remorse, blame, shame, guilt and a myriad of emotions, and when faced with the choice between moving forward, or punishing yourself, you may opt for the latter.

Show me a person who hasn't experienced loss, disappointment and their fair share of eff ups and you'll be showing me someone who is either head deep in denial or hasn't lived and grown.

What I have learned is that you don't have to tell anyone that you 'forgive' them, but what's more important is to forgive yourself because often we're secretly most angry with ourselves, even if that anger is misplaced. We're angry for not being able to control something, for not having the last word, for making mistakes, for not treating ourselves as we should, and for not being able to change the past. Sometimes we're angry for still being angry. You have to forgive you. If you think forgiveness is going to tap you on the shoulder one day after you've spent sufficient time punishing yourself and ruminating the crap out of past experiences, you'll be in for a long wait.

Forgiveness is a choice and a decision undertaken by you. Forgiveness is

an action.

Being angry, frustrated and disappointed with you, and torturing yourself with guilt, blame, and shame causes you the most pain, just like when you hold onto anger about others, it's only you that it affects.

You have to make a decision to offload the burden of all of these feelings so that you can move forward. It's a choice between remaining in a comfort zone of punishment and emotional purgatory, or change.

You have to choose to forgive you – no ifs, buts or maybes.

The way to offload all of this 'stuff' that's hanging around is to park it in the past and the way to park it in the past is to commit to quitting relationship insanity. It is the commitment to not continuing to carry the same baggage, belief, and behaviours, and reflecting this in your subsequent actions, thinking, and experiences, that will separate you from your past and create growth.

'But, but, if I let it go, then it's final, I have to accept reality and I have to deal with myself!' you might be thinking.

The thing about punishing yourself, holding onto anger, and remaining stuck in this fantasy, is that it gives you a purpose while also acting as a barrier to actually having to take steps in your own life and exact change. Letting go of the anger and forgiving yourself does mean taking them down off their gilded pedestal and seeing them in reality, which will burst the bubble of the fantasy. It means having to be present, having to think of you, maybe suddenly finding that you don't think about him that much, and recognising that much of the reason why you are being kept down is because you are keeping you down with the burden of all of this fantasising and punishment. Take it away and you have to rise into yourself. You have to find something better to do with your time, and like most people with low self-esteem, while you'll break your neck liking and trying to please others, you often have no clue where to start when it comes to being good to yourself. It's like you don't know what to do if it doesn't involve sinking energy into external sources of validation.

It's time to stop avoiding yourself. It's time to stop avoiding life. It's time to have a more meaningful purpose that enriches your life. It's time to stop holding you down. It's time to let go.

COMMIT TO SELF-LOVE

People like to think there's something complicated about making a commitment to love yourself – there isn't. You have to choose and keep choosing day after day after day to treat you with love, care, trust and respect. It's easy to get caught up in the fact that you have a habit of not loving you – we all have to start from somewhere. It doesn't matter where, it just matters that you start and continue.

Self-esteem is a combination of minuscule, small, medium and large acts and thoughts. It is not automatic and you won't generate instant results, but history has taught you that searching for instant results and quick fixes doesn't benefit beyond the moment and the short-term.

Self-esteem also means that you have to act in your own best interests, even when it means making uncomfortable decisions, seeing things as they are and opting out, even when your hopes and libido may say differently.

Create boundaries so that you know, communicate and act upon your limits, understand unhealthy behaviours, ask questions, act upon feedback, accept no lies, denials and excuses, and show you that you can be trusted by showing up every day to look out for you. Admit when you've made mistakes, don't be afraid to judge situations, live – these all show that you're a person who can be trusted, in particular by you. There are tips and tools on all of these areas in *Mr Unavailable and the Fallback Girl* and on my site www.baggagereclaim.com.

WRITE UNSENT LETTERS

Write out your anger so that you can organise your thoughts and process how you feel. It will help you to distinguish between your anger towards you, including misplaced anger and anger towards others, plus it can help you piece together the chain of events and put some closure and perspective on your feelings. A very healing, productive exercise, write without restraint and pour out what's on your mind – until you do, the toxicity can keep you stuck in your feelings and in a fantasy. It can also be very helpful to write several letters over a period of time, that, when you read them back at a later date (if you choose to), will show your growth in perspective and healing. You may even find it helpful to destroy the letter in a demonstration of letting go. There are tips on this in *Mr Unavailable and the Fallback Girl* plus a detailed free guide on my site.

LETTERS TO YOURSELF

Self-esteem can involve you acting like a best friend to yourself. You may find that you're able to be far more compassionate, empathetic, and full of support and advice for others but struggle to apply it in your own life due to being your harshest critic.

Write letters to yourself either as a best friend, you speaking to your younger self, or you just being very straight with you. Whichever option you take, even though you will likely address where you've erred, it is overall a positive letter to you. This also gives you a good opportunity to deal with feedback that you may not want to hear (criticism) and see it, not as punishment, but honesty with respect and an opportunity to hear something that you can learn positively from. The compassion, never-ending understanding, empathy, kindness, love, care, trust, respect, forgiveness and chances that you dole out to others, must now be directed at you.

Don't use the letters as an opportunity to punish you and wallow in more blame and shame – see the commitment to the letter through and choose a role (best friend, you speaking to a younger you, or straight no chaser you) that you can assume and embrace the task of being supportive.

- What would a best friend say? A best friend, while they will tell you the situation as it is and offer support, won't berate or judge you.

- What can you say to help grow up a younger you so that you can make better, mature, more realistic choices? You have the benefit of hindsight and experience – demonstrate what you have learned. And no, you wouldn't say, 'Don't bother with love!' or condemn a younger you.

- Given an opportunity to be real with no fantasy bubble around you, what would you say? Show that you can be honest with respect. No berating, scolding, punishment, ridicule etc., although you may find that you can suddenly see the funnier side of life and be gentler with you.

Write without editing, censorship and fear – shoot straight from the hip and the heart and don't read back. Put it in an envelope and seal it straight away. If after you put it in the envelope, you think of something else to say, start a new letter. It's also best to write when you know you won't be interrupted for at least half an hour.

And yes, you do have time – if you've had time to live in your unconscious chasing fantasy relationships and ruminating over what you think your flaws and screw ups are, you have time to write a letter – lots of them. These are a more productive use of your energy that engages you with reality.

Start with a recent experience that has really affected you as the basis for

the letter. It may be a date or a relationship not fulfilling the hopes and expectations you had, or an issue with family, a misunderstanding with a friend, or something you worked hard on not getting the response you had expected. If you try to cover your whole life in one letter, you may feel overwhelmed – if you'd like to work through a number of experiences, either start most recent and work back, or start from the beginning and work up and do it in a series of letters instead of the one. This can be a great way of getting to know you and understanding what's been lingering in your mind.

If you've pissed yourself off, put it all in there... then give yourself some perspective, compassion and some supportive advice.

- What is the stuff that you know has really derailed you?
- Where have you deviated from your values?
- Where have you deviated from what you know to be right or even good for you?
- Where have you procrastinated?
- Where have you compromised yourself? Been self-indulgent?
- Where have you been stubborn?

Your support must be based in answering the question: What can I do differently that will support me as an individual, meaning that I can live in line with my values, treat me with love, care, trust and respect so that I feel valued, worthwhile and more confident in my interactions?

What new actions will you commit to? Tie these in with the life you desire to create.

When you're done with each letter, either put them away for safekeeping. You don't need to read them straight away, but when you do feel a wobble, take them out and read them to remind yourself of the self-supportive voice that resides within you. You can of course always post them to yourself – you may want to wait a few days and then send it in the slowest mail that you can. It may help to number each envelope e.g. #1 so that when you decide to read through them, you can immediately know what order to start in.

The purpose of the letter to yourself is to feel better, to cleanse yourself of toxic thoughts and give you the foundations and stepping stones for creating action and purpose in your life. The letter(s) and ultimately the forgiveness you grant yourself is also a gift – grab it with both hands.

DROPPING THE WALLS TO OVERCOME YOUR FEAR OF INTIMACY

Everyone has some level of fear about being emotionally vulnerable and committed. Everyone. The difference between you and someone who is experiencing genuine intimacy and commitment is that they experience these feelings but do it anyway with a foundation of mutual love, care, trust, respect and reality. These people are no 'better' than you and actually, for all you know, some of them may have dealt with worse or similar experiences to you – they're still standing and trying.

Attempting to have a relationship without genuine intimacy is like walking around with a force field around you – you're limiting how much you can feel, how close you can get to people and locking out key elements of a relationship.

Feel all of your feelings – good, bad and indifferent. Don't run from them and instead of shutting down anything that's uncomfortable and painful by fantasising or engaging in destructive behaviour and thinking, whether it's alone or with somebody else, let the feelings happen, process and work through them. Make sure you expand your range of feelings – many unavailable people seem to use 'hurt' as a general descriptor for their emotional reaction to any experience that they don't like. Keep a Feelings Diary so you can get a sense of when you feel good (or bad) and what triggers it. This is basically noting your moods and the shifts in them in a journal or notebook. They are great for identifying associations and triggers that prompt feelings, thoughts and subsequent actions and you will soon see a clear pattern. You can find help on this on my site www.baggagereclaim.com.

Change your labels and descriptors. A barrier to intimacy is already having a negative association with particular emotions that may actually represent a mislabelling. For example, experiencing sadness, disappointment, frustration, rejection, stress, pressure, uncertainty, ambiguity, conflict may automatically be associated with something that you've previously ascribed to it – something being wrong with you, inadequacy, a 'failure' on your part, the onset of doom etc. These are likely learned associations from childhood or that you've at least held for a lengthy period of time, that they're second nature, which means that they require you to be conscious and start listening to and challenging you to not default to self-blame. As a result of the automatic negative association, of course you going to want to avoid these feelings but actually, it's that you need to actually feel them and recognise the incorrect labelling and association.

Keep a list of what you feel and what the contributing factors were in a Feelings Diary and question the feeling – is there another word that you could use to describe it?

Match what you say and think with your actions. This enables you to be authentic. You cannot live congruently with yourself when you think one thing, say another, and do something else entirely. You communicate that you're a jumbled up person but also, being out of sync blocks the opportunity to be honest which automatically creates walls. I realised that I cannot expect honesty, nor claim to be honest, if, not only do I lie to myself, but I involve myself in an affair. I also can't expect to be happy and in a progressing relationship if I'm with someone who already is with someone else! Look at where your life contradicts what you profess to think, need and want – this is where you can make change and communicate more clearly about yourself.

You don't have to chase each feeling, especially with negativity. There's definitely a pervasive attitude with unavailable people, of 'I had a feeling, I must go after it, give room to it, and pile on a whole load of meaning.' You don't have to chase after every feeling and give it credence, especially if what you pile onto it is rumination and feeling 'not good enough'. This doesn't mean shutting down your feelings, or not feeling them, but you don't have to chase after negative feelings with, 'Yeah, I'm no good', or 'Yeah, this is all my fault', or 'I feel like this because I'm not worthy of XYZ.' You could feel sad, angry, frustrated, disappointed, wistful and even regretful without following it up with some self-persecution that will only accentuate whatever you're feeling.

You also don't have to chase every feeling with destruction. 'I feel bored... Oh, I'll text my batshit ex', or 'I feel lonely... Oh, it's because I'm no good... I'll just head into town and hit up someone for some random sex so that I can feel better', 'I miss my ex... Oh, remember when we did this... and remember when we did that... it doesn't matter that they did XYZ... I miss them so it must mean I love them and should be with them... right I'm sending a text/email/dialling them repeatedly/showing up in a fur coat and no knickers. 'You got all of that from a feeling?

Again, it's not about avoiding your feelings, but it is about not shutting down a feeling and avoiding questioning it, and instead opting to engage in destructive behaviour that actually has nothing to do with the feeling. If you're bored with your own company, find things to do that help you to enjoy your own company. Learn to understand your feelings instead of soothing them with destructive whims and negative thinking.

Don't overshare. There is a danger with having walls but wanting to suss out your 'opponent', to then wear your heart and hurt on your sleeve and disclose all of your fears, pain, past etc. For a start, it would be better to get a handle on your fears, grieve your losses/resolve old hurt and ensure that your past is not your present, but you also need to share appropriately.

This isn't about being secretive but it is about getting to know someone in reality at a pace that gives you room to see, hear and feel before you 'spill'. People who overshare do so because it also helps to create a faux connection and faux intimacy. Unfortunately, by not entering into dating with a reasonable level of trust, going through the discovery process of dating, then crediting your 'trust account' for positive signs and debiting for negative, oversharing is like giving someone the blueprints to screw you over. Then you'll go, 'I knew that people can't be trusted' – no, it's that you shouldn't overshare to create false trust – share because there is trust and you're doing it without an agenda. Trust is a stepping stone to intimacy. Faux trust is a stepping stone to pain, which will only cause you to put up more defensive walls. If this stuff is so present that you feel you need to warn them, it's not old stuff – it's present and needs to be dealt with.

Minimise the amount of time you spend trying to anticipate what's next and worrying about what might or isn't happening – mindfulness. It's difficult to be genuinely authentic and intimate when you're in another world. Devoting so much energy to thinking ahead and worrying not only affects your actions but also throws up walls. This anticipation and worry is a brutal mix of query and suspicion. It's like you can't trust and handle what's going on. You want to know what the next act is, you want to speed things up so that it can either fuck up or give you the great fantasy.

Spending a lot of time being afraid gives you no choice but to be unable to use the trust you should have built up in someone, or trust yourself. On one hand you don't want the fear to be correct and on the other hand, you don't want to think you're expending this energy for nothing. The present needs you and when you are not devoting so much of your mental energy to being out of it, you are here to feel your feelings, live and appreciate your experiences, and address any actual concerns.

If you have the time to devote to anticipating and worrying, you are eroding a fledgling intimacy between you both. You're not metaphorically looking them in the eye – you're looking over their shoulder and into the skies, plus you're also watching your back and being on high alert. Intimacy requires presentness.

Don't try to 'matchmake' your walls with someone else's. Unavailable relationships prevent intimacy, so if you find yourself in a situation that has the hallmarks of an unavailable relationship, take it as a code red alerting you to abort mission. Don't try to scale their walls on a love mission – not only is it a waste of your energy but you'll actually alienate yourself and bust their boundaries. If you meet walls you will find that you have to have walls in order to engage at their level because you have to shut down your feelings and needs.

Assess the danger. Fear is an emotional response to a perceived threat. While of course the person who you're involved with may represent a 'threat', fear of intimacy is also tied to old threats which means that the walls are up anyway regardless of an existing threat or not. It is critical to make sure you have merit based fear and that when there are genuine reasons to be concerned, that you respond with action.

Stop, look, listen and assess and address the concern, and don't proceed if you haven't.

This means assessing whether it's an internal or external fear – is this about your own existing fears and insecurities that you may have in fact shown up to a situation with, or is the other party behaving in ways that should be a cause for a concern?

Drop the assumptions. Even though it may be subconscious, if you use assumptions as a basis for your thinking, on some level you accept that there's a distinct possibility that you're barking up the wrong tree which starts to add bricks on to your walls. Dropping the assumptions forces you to have an honest conversation with yourself as well as engaging in honest conversations with others, which brings me neatly to…

Be respectfully direct instead of hinting. Intimacy cannot go anywhere without communication. If you hint and go round the houses expecting people to figure out what it is you feel, expect or need based on your vibe, vaguely alluding, or the almost constipated facial expression, you and they will end up missing the point entirely.

Hinting is for surprises, such as birthday gifts, not for letting someone know how you feel, or what you want, need or expect. The fact that you would drop hints and rely on them communicates that you don't trust them or yourself, to take the basic risk of sharing what's on your mind.

Hinting is a cornerstone of intimacy lacking relationships.

Equally the whole hanging around being helpful or looking doe-eyed at them, sleeping with them, being their friend and all that jazz – this is not direct communication, especially if you end up piling on your feelings without clarifying that you're in a mutual situation.

Hinting is handy for minimising the risk of rejection but this ends up being a false economy, because people invariably don't get the hint (or choose not to) and if you don't heed this, you can end up feeling rejected, hurt, taken advantage of or even abused.

Recognise that when walls are removed, there's freedom and opportunity for happiness. Many of the people who get in touch with me about experiences stress how lonely and neglected they are, with struggling friendships as well as issues with family often punctuating their relationship experiences. Part of leading a more enriched and rewarding life is putting yourself out there, which involves risk, and by taking down your walls, you can foster stronger, healthier, mutual connections.

You can communicate all the wrong things about yourself when you spend your time limiting your experiences so that you don't run the risk of anything unpleasant. You want to meet people as an equal – you've got to step into their world and they yours. Mutual relationships can't have pussyfooting – if you meet people with walls and engage in behaviour that attempts to reduce rejection etc, your unwillingness to communicate, to have boundaries, to express displeasure, to express anything, will limit your relationships. Walls and happiness don't mix, so unburden yourself.

Grieve your previous losses. I find that the biggest walls created seem to have their foundations and the bricks laid upon them from previous relationships and painful experiences that you're not at peace with. I talk to some readers who are not emotionally over exes that run into double digits – they're still angry, hurt, or even hoping that a significant portion of these people will make good on the previous poor experience. It's bad enough struggling to get over one person, but to carry around anger, frustrations and hurt over several, or even twenty, thirty exes is burdensome. Carrying pain over an extended period of time is burdensome and will affect you more than anyone else. This is where you will find that *Unsent Letters, Letters To Yourself* and potentially spending time with a therapist or attending support groups, will help bring your grief up to the surface and out, instead of bubbling underneath and eating away at you. Be prepared to feel worse before you feel good, but recognise that if you feel crappy with it coming out of you, how much damage you're doing internally by holding it in.

If you've been thinking that time is a great healer, you're probably wondering why the hell you're still bothered about and affected by all of this stuff – it's what you do with the time. I've found that many of my readers have recognised the passage of time as being a catalyst for hurling themselves back out there into a new experience – burying feelings, repeating unhealthy patterns, or using new behaviour based on your unresolved feelings are a recipe for pain.

I've also heard from many readers who have huge gaps between their relationships. They expected time to heal and in the meantime felt so cut up about the loss, that next thing you know, 5, 6, 7, 8, 9, 10 or even more years had gone by. Again the feelings were buried but they weren't healed. It's also a hell of a lot of time to think about loss and be angry. It's not that you need to be over something in quick time and depending on what the nature of a loss is, it may take a longer to get over due to the trauma – but time is not going to fix it.

You can give yourself some time to start to come to terms with the loss and work your way through denial, anger, bargaining, depression and acceptance but if you rely on time to sweep you away and you're already inclined to be lost in your unconscious and to give yourself a hard time, what you really need to do is find additional means of support, such as the letters, the therapy, re-integrating into life, investing in yourself. Time itself isn't really going to do anything if your mind and body aren't moving with it in a positive direction.

Question and separate out your grief – get to the heart of what's really bothering you. What many people who have been stuck on the loss of someone following a breakup, traumatic experience etc find, is, yes, they're upset about it, but many of the feelings and thoughts that they're stuck on have very little to do with the actual grief related to the breakup or the experience. When I speak with readers about why they feel so angry, hurt and stuck, what I hear is:

- Anger with yourself.
- Fear of starting over.
- Fear of being alone.
- Boredom – not knowing what to do with yourself.
- Regret, or even blame and shame for the things you wish you coulda, woulda, shoulda done.
- Not wanting to see the truth about yourself or others.
- Memories of other painful experiences.

- Feeling like you've lost your purpose.
- Unresolved grief from a bereavement.
- Anger with people you feel haven't supported you.

While these may be related in some way to the grief, in that this current experience has resurrected old feelings, they're not the same as, for example, the grief related to this breakup. That's why it becomes difficult to get out of feeling stuck – because you're blocked from dealing with this current loss by previous unresolved losses. When you address these other experiences and feelings, you can be realistic about where you're stuck, where you're at, and where you're going to. From personal experience, when I broke up with one ex, it turned out it wasn't really about him; it was grief to do with my father and my childhood. When I acknowledged this and gradually dealt with it, it allowed me to see my loss of the ex more clearly and with fresh perspective.

You cannot change any of the experiences – the split has still happened, someone has disappointed you, and you can't get into a time machine and undo certain things that you've done. What you can do, by allowing your feelings and grief to come to the surface and be acknowledged, felt, and dealt with, is you can change the meaning that you attach to these experiences (for example, them being some damning indictment of you as a person) and your perception of them – with time, hindsight and reality comes fresh perspective.

LET GO OF BEING A

PERFECTIONIST BLAME

ABSORBER

It is an illusion to think that you are safer with your 'contained' risks because the person who you most need to change your relationship with and be more compassionate to, is you. This isn't to say that you haven't had painful experiences, however, most of this negative dialogue is between you, yourself, and you.

Never, ever, ever, ever, ever take sole responsibility for something that was not wholly and solely within your control. Ever.

You see how you've been looking for 'perfection' and trying to avoid so many different things? Well, when you have a habit of making things about you, which is inverted ego issues, it's also a perfectionism issue.

As a Dreamer, you're either taking responsibility for everything (blaming and shaming), which is actually just another means of lying to yourself and remaining invested in a fantasy, albeit a negative one, or you're avoiding responsibility altogether and putting it all on everyone else (denial). In fact, you may even be more concerned with having the last word and fighting for something that you don't actually want and is working against you, but you don't want anymore blemishes on your 'record'.

In the real world, which is where you're actually based and supposed to be, the truth, especially when there is more than one person involved, is somewhere in between perfection – reality. What's yours is yours, what's theirs is theirs.

Take responsibility for specific actions that you can with a high degree of certainty demonstrate that there is a specific cause and effect in play, but do not generalise what you perceive to be your 'inadequacies' and use them as a blanket to throw over everything that goes wrong in your life, especially Other People's Behaviour. It's bullshit to go, 'Relationship didn't work out; I'm not good enough', 'They didn't call; they've figured out that I'm not good enough', 'They didn't do/say as I wanted/expected, I'm not good enough', because what needs to end is the central theme of not being good enough, which would give way to actually seeing things in reality and recognising the contributions of others as well as yourself, instead of being an equal opportunity blame absorber.

If your supposed fuck ups make you 'rejectionable' and the other person is fucking up no matter how much you try to blow smoke up their arse and put them on a pedestal, but yet you still blame yourself not only for your own actions but for theirs, it means you're saddling up with other people's rejection. This is not just hard labour; it's punishment and an unnecessary one at that.

If the person has also behaved in ways that, at best, take advantage of you and at their worst, involve you being abused, you absolutely must not take responsibility for their actions – it's what they thrive on to keep you under their control and 'useful'.

They're behaving as they do anyway – this is their inclination and you haven't created new behaviour in them that's inspired by some flaw in you. Of course there are things that you can do so that you are not involved with them in the first place or you cut and run as soon as their behaviour becomes apparent, but that's very different to pondering why you were rejected by someone who is abusing you and wondering how to gain acceptance – you should be looking for an exit.

Yes people do make decisions that you don't like about dating and relationships. What you should recognise is that people make these decisions that affect us based on superficial reasons, personal unrelated reasons, personal related reasons, incompatible values, characteristics and qualities, feelings or a lack of them, perceptions of love, relationships, themselves and possibly you, mood, horniness, the grass is greener, stress, pressure, pain, shortcomings, poor judgement, and many more. That right there is a long list of reasons, and it's egotistical to ignore everything else and home-in on the 'you' part and then make yourself responsible for 'everything'.

You do, or at least have in the past, made these decisions too – I'd like to think that you're not hoping that someone would eat away at themselves and throw away their lives due to any judgement you made, because you're not supposed to be that powerful. They aren't that powerful either.

If a person ever shares their reasons, there is also a distinct possibility that there is an element, or even a lot, of untruth, because they either want to avoid conflict or want to avoid any personal responsibility. This is most definitely the case when you're dealing with someone who you already had a relationship tinged, or even chock full, with bullshit – it's quite ridiculous to be involved with someone and choose not to believe them when they, for example, say, 'I'm not ready for a relationship', so that you can proceed with the fantasy, and then when it's over, decide that 'suddenly' every word you didn't believe previously is now gospel and that as a result of what they've claimed are their reasons for how they've treated you, that you're not good enough.

You may rationalise that it turns out that they weren't lying then so it means that their reasoning for their subsequent behaviour or it not working out, that they may be pinning on you, is true. What you forget is that while they may not have been lying about that, their actions and words haven't matched and in order to maintain their own position, they're often very economical with the truth. In turn, dabbling with truth as a get out clause for when things go tits up further down the line, helps them to absolve themselves of responsibility.

Prime example: They say, 'I don't want a relationship right now. Let's just keep this casual.' You say, 'But I want more, so I don't think I can do this.' They appear to respect your wishes and then start calling, texting or trying to sleep with you, or they just carry on as normal and expect you to either sign on or jog on. If you stick around, you think, 'Well, I know they said that they don't want a relationship but surely if this was the case and they know how I feel, they wouldn't want to keep hanging out, sleeping together or sexting me?' They think, 'Well, they're obviously OK with what I've said and, at the end of the day, if they're not, I'll remind them that I did say that I didn't want a relationship, so if they wanted more, they should have left.' And bingo, responsibility gone. Next thing you know, you're wondering what you did for them to say that they don't want a relationship in the first place and blaming yourself, and then you're blaming yourself for not being patient or it not working out.

The whole thing is a lie, that, yes, you participated in but they lied and economised with information while contradicting with their actions.

If you have to be responsible for the outcome of the relationship. So. Do. They.

Due to people's bias towards remaining in their comfort zones, it means you have a greater duty of care to work out who you are and get to a reasonable level of self-esteem before you participate in dating because, due to the very nature of it, you are likely to experience 'rejection', no matter how much you try to avoid it. Getting a reasonable handle on your identity means that you can maintain a separate identity and not run around owning others' identities or what they project onto you.

IDENTIFY THE BLOCKS

There is a very specific reason why people either blame themselves for everything or deny all responsibility, and it's because, in doing so, they avoid seeing and hearing 'unpleasant' things, whether it's about their own culpability including the choices and mentality that have contributed, or the other person's.

The moment that you identify what it is that you're truly avoiding hearing and seeing, is the moment that you move into a position of being responsible and accountable.

What are the specific things that you feel you gain by either blaming yourself, or putting it all on them?

- What does it distract you from? Whatever it's distracting you from is actually where you should be putting your energy.

- What specific behaviours and incidences do you overlook? These may be things that you overlook in yourself, or it may be in them. Often, these things are overlooked so that excuses that you've made remain intact and don't put you in the position of taking action and making uncomfortable decisions. This is particularly relevant to you if you tend to focus on 'good points' or 'good times'.

- What choices that you're secretly feeling regretful about, do you get to avoid? When you feel bad about procrastinating, or selling yourself short, or doing something that was way outside of your values, it can seem easier to focus on something else than take on the full force of the truth and handle feeling regretful.

- If you weren't taking all the blame, what would you have to face about the other person? What are you pushing down about them? What are you sacrificing yourself for so that your image of them can remain intact?

Explore these specifics and write them down so that they get out of your head and onto paper so that they become real. When you examine these 'gains' that you felt you were making, how many of them are actually gains? When you consider how you feel right now and have been feeling, has what you've been doing actually been working for you? While I appreciate that, in the short-term, it is uncomfortable to let go of old habits, use the truth of the results to accept that how you do things isn't working and address what you've been avoiding.

Why are you taking all the blame? List the reasons no matter how 'silly' you think they may be.

- How many of these relate to specific actions taken or specific incidences in this relationship?
- How many of the reasons relate to past relationships and experiences?
- How many of these relate to general opinions you hold about yourself that determine what you regard as your worth as a person?
- How many regard inadequacies that you already believed that you had anyway?

Looking at your reasons for taking the blame, how many of these are accurate, factual and reasonable? What you invariably discover when you list all of the reasons for taking the blame, is that the reasons are unrealistic and unreasonable. That's why you're stuck. When people are responsible and accountable, while it's not to say that they don't experience painful consequences, they move on from them due to being accountable and responsible, and so having to reflect what they've learned into their future actions. Your experiences post blame are showing you that absorbing all of the blame isn't working for you and is in fact opening you up to further pain.

What do you think you should have been or should have done to not experience this outcome? List the reasons.

I should have said…

I should have done…

I should have been…
I should have tried…
I should have made sure that…
I should be…

Then question each one. Why should you have said something? Why should you have done something? Is it irrefutably true that if all of your 'shoulds' had happened, that you would have experienced a different outcome? How can it be? It's only you that you have control over. If they were behaving in ways that were not conducive to a mutually fulfilling relationship, that's on them, not you.

When you examine the reasons for why you're taking the blame, you will see that you are responding to very little of the relationship itself, and very much to how you feel about you. You might even be responding to past experiences but what you're not responding to is *this* problem and *this* situation plus you're putting too much of you in it – you are claiming control and influence over another person that you don't possess. It's also important to recognise that taking the blame for something because of a previous experience, is really just flogging yourself for something that's already been and gone – yep, punishing yourself all over again.

Being under illusions about why something went wrong or what your part was, sets you up to continue to never truly gain anything out of your experiences and move on. Take all your 'I should…' from above and turn it around so that you take your power back and change the meaning of these experiences.

When you realise that you don't need to be _____ [insert whatever unhealthy belief such as change their values, make them leave someone, make them change their mind about committing, dialalay.com] in order to be a great partner or good enough for _____, because you already are, you stop doing things that make you feel bad in an attempt to feel good.

For example: When you realise that you don't need to be a doormat in order to be great partner, you recognise that you're good enough anyway, live authentically, and recognise the inappropriateness of someone expecting you to offload your boundaries.

Or, when you realise that you don't need to put up with being treated in a less than manner in order to be good enough for commitment and effort, you recognise that you're good enough anyway and show up with boundaries and an immovable expectation of being treated decently at all times, no exceptions.

ROLE PLAY

Let's 'pretend' for a few minutes that you're not all the things that you consciously and subconsciously believe you are. Let's take all the reasons you've just come up with, throw them aside and imagine that you are a 100% worthy person who owns their behaviour, lets the other party own theirs and doesn't blame themselves for anything that is not wholly and solely down to them. How does the same situation look?

Example: With your fur coat of denial on

If I had been good enough and just loved him enough, we would still be together. The fact that he didn't make an effort and, in fact, gradually withdrew and rationed down his initial efforts, happened because he gradually saw something in me that confirmed that he shouldn't commit to me. I tried so hard to be and do what he wants and changed myself so much – it was never enough and it has to be because I'm not enough of a person.

Example: With your new perspective

Even though I am good enough, we wouldn't be together. The amount of effort that he made was down to him. I'm not suggesting that I'm perfect, but I don't deserve to be neglected and mistreated by anyone. He withdrew because he was unavailable and he was never planning on sticking around. I wanted him to be different and to make me the exception. Really, I could have twisted myself into a pretzel, and it still wouldn't have been enough because his problem with committing is about him, just like my problem with committing is about me. I tried and tried and it had little impact, so to think that if it had been enough, he would have spontaneously treated me better, is to ignore the fact that he didn't. Also, when someone has changed their mind about committing, they should move on, just like I should have moved on instead of sticking with the fantasy.

Your discoveries about your part in your relationship experiences aren't there as an opportunity to blame yourself, but to empower you to recognise what isn't working and to make changes. Stop taking responsibility for 'everything'; start taking responsibility for you.

GETTING OVER 'DISAPPROVAL' & CONFLICT

For most of my life, I feared criticism and conflict, because there was a lot of it as a child. My takeaway message of not living up to someone's expectations or getting something wrong, or whatever it was that caused an expression of disapproval, is 'I'm a failure' and I figured that when I was good enough and the relationship was 'right', criticism and conflict wouldn't exist. Once you start internalising any and all forms of 'disapproval' and disagreement as a veto of you as a person, you'll default to being afraid of the perceived onset of criticism and conflict, adapting your behaviour in advance, in an effort to dodge them, and then being hypersensitive to it and reacting, often quickly and without consideration.

I'm not saying that I now love criticism and I still have to give myself a boot up the bum sometimes to face potential conflict, but certainly over the past six years or so, I really don't give a rats as much as I used to. The consequences of internalisation or compromising myself are far greater than any criticism or conflict I might experience.

I know when to see opportunities and feedback in 'criticism', and I also know when to mentally give someone the two fingers. Equally, I also see any conflict that does arise as an opportunity – either way I'm going to come out of it with knowledge. What I can tell you with absolute certainty, is that you can handle disapproval and conflict. You can. The sky isn't going to fall in if you don't please everyone or even someone you really like, because you can't please everyone all of the time. You're not pleased all of the time – no one is!

There are a number of things that can change the meaning of 'criticism' and conflict for you and allow you retain your sense of self so that you don't spiral.

You receive 'feedback', both positive and negative, not just verbally or through people's actions, but from life itself. When you keep experiencing the same situations, it's life throwing up the same lessons until you learn them. It may seem like 'negative' feedback initially, because you may experience what appears to be an unfavourable result, but it then paves the way to positive feedback through the subsequent results and lessons learned.

You can only learn to handle criticism and feedback with reality which gives perspective. Reduce the impact by sticking to the facts and keeping your feet in reality. Force the illusions out of your life bit by bit and stop looking for reasons to feel unworthy.

Change the meaning of criticism from 'I'm not good enough', or 'I'm a failure' to 'Someone is asking me to listen…' If you don't, you'll focus on bathing in a sense of inadequacy and withdraw into yourself.

Listening doesn't mean agreement and criticism doesn't equate to 'I must change to stop disapproval.' If you start listening and the person becomes disrespectful, or even abusive, you're free to end the conversation and walk away.

Sometimes, in fact, often, what you perceive as a potential conflict really isn't. It's important to calm down and not let yourself get carried away with what you think that the other person is thinking or over-investing your time and energy into formulating a response or even a 'defence'.

Even if feedback is negative, if you can look beyond your nose and

recognise the lesson, whether it's from the feedback itself or what receiving it means about the person/situation, you only stand to gain. In relationships, you sometimes find that at the time, due to your ego feeling a bit dented, you weren't ready to hear the feedback or see what it meant, but it may make sense at a later date. Yes you could have heeded it sooner, but what matters is that you have. Sometimes when partners say stuff, all it does confirm is that you're not who they say you are, but that they really don't know you – that is a red flag, especially if what they're saying actually cuts you down. Your job is not to prove them wrong – it's to tell them to jog on.

Criticism isn't the same as disapproval of you as a person or rejection. Listen to the feedback. Is it actually a message saying that you are a less than person? Or is that how you see it? If you equate conflict or hearing something that you don't want to as disapproval, you're seeing the monster in everything, even when there isn't and they're just telling you where they think you could do better or that something isn't working for them.

Let this idea go that experiencing conflict is a sign that you've done something 'wrong'. It could easily be the other person, or both of you having a misunderstanding, or something of nothing. You don't get to know this if you're already going, 'Wah, wah, wah, it's me!'

Criticism and conflict also doesn't mean that a relationship is over or on the way to being so. Part of being a mature adult in a relationship is being able to have a disagreement or not always hear what you want to hear, and not put the relationship in jeopardy each time. You're then both free to be available and truly intimate with one another.

Someone's criticism isn't always accurate or the right thing for you. You can listen to it, let it percolate, consider the suggestions and look at where it fits with your agenda and your values, and then choose a course of action that's right for you.

Let me assure you: Any form of 'feedback' that involves you screwing yourself over while busting up your boundaries and values, is not in your best interests.

If you focus mostly on the criticism and your stinging reaction to it, you'll fail to see the wood for the trees. You may miss a valuable opportunity to learn something very key about you or the situation that would pave the way to better experiences, even if it's without them.

Criticism or feedback, is not an opportunity to be disrespectful or even abusive. It's not a free pass on decency. When done in a mean-spirited or abusive manner it's their character.

'Who are you to judge?' should help you work out in your mind whether the person is qualified to critique you. If they are someone who has consistently treated you with care, trust and respect, or a customer, or you know there's a genuine basis for the criticism, hear them out.

If they are someone who claims to be trying to help you and being 'honest', while being dishonest about their own part or even deluded about who they are, they are not qualified to be telling you who you are or giving you improvement tips.

Accept that you cannot like or love 'everything', just like you cannot be liked and loved by 'everyone'. If you have this burning desire to gain someone's approval, question it. What do you think you're going to experience? What do you think it will tell you about you? It's unlikely to be for rational reasons and needing and seeking it, immediately puts them on a pedestal. Take 'em off!

Even when you do express actual disapproval or they do, it's not the end of life as you know it. Maybe you don't like something, maybe something brings out a far stronger reaction, such as disgust, displeasure, dissatisfaction, or a very strong verbal or physical objection. Whatever the disapproval is, it doesn't put a final judgement on someone. What it may do is show a difference in values, which means you're incompatible. Buh-bye!

When you refuse to accept feedback and, yes, at times, criticism, you're saying, 'I have nothing to learn' and 'You cannot say anything that I don't like because you'll upset me.' No relationship of any kind, romantic or otherwise, can progress even an inch without the room for respectful feedback and, at times, yes, criticism. Nobody wants to tiptoe. It's a fantasy to believe that love is never hearing feedback or criticism and that you can aim for a life where you never experience it.

When you accept that you can and will experience it, you can prepare positively for it, by having the self-esteem and perspective to take it.

Don't react immediately. That means don't blame yourself immediately, don't start running yourself down with internal criticism, don't immediately attempt to compromise, don't grovel, don't do a thing. Unless you're in a dangerous situation, which means you should be exiting pronto, listen without throwing all of your stuff into the pot and give it consideration. One of the first things you'll learn by not having an instant reaction and running with it is that the sky doesn't fall down and whatever you think that the worst is, isn't happening. Don't reply (if you're face to face) until you've taken a few breaths, relaxed into yourself and feel a bit more balanced. Definitely don't fire off texts or emails in anger.

If you immediately react angrily or defensively, you'll likely end up feeling regretful and then believing that the criticism or manner of conflict was justified, even if it wasn't. You'll then focus on your reaction and making amends for that, instead of the issue at hand.

Not everyone who gives criticism is out to 'get' you. There are plenty of celebrities on this planet who are living examples of what happens when you don't feel that you need 'feedback' and everyone tells you what you want to hear. When something drastic happens, due to being shrouded in cotton wool, they react very badly. Next thing, they've spiralled into addiction or attacking everyone for not telling them the truth sooner.

Someone who adds value to your life will bite the bullet and say the necessary and the uncomfortable because they want to see you succeed. You'll also find that someone who is genuinely offering you feedback isn't basing the need to or desired outcome on something to do with them. In a relationship, if they're an available, mature individual, in a situation you've both been involved in, they'll discuss their part and look at ways that you can both help your relationship or situation succeed.

Make sure you manage your 'frequencies' and 'filters'. Short of running off every time you sense criticism, you will have to experience and handle it. How much of a negative impact it makes on you, and what you stand to gain (if anything), is greatly altered by ensuring that you know who to tune into and who to filter out their crap.

Someone who has, at best, taken advantage of and, at worst, abused you, is someone that you need to tune out of, because they don't have your best interests at heart; what they have is their agenda. Someone who embodies healthy values and lives their life authentically is someone you can tune into. That said, after you tune in, you have to use your filters to get to the heart of the message and grab the information that you can use.

Just because someone does give you feedback though, it doesn't mean that you have to implement it. It's feedback, not a directive or a court order. This isn't to say that whenever you do get feedback that you've got to say, 'Eff it in a bucket and chuck it', and continue down a destructive path, but what it does mean is that you must remember that you are the person who is in charge of your life. Give careful consideration to 'structural' and behavioural changes, plus you cannot change for every single person that feels like giving some input into your life.

When you deem that someone disapproves of you, whether it's because they're not interested, or they make a criticism, or they don't want the relationship that you want, that doesn't mean that you are unacceptable. They're just one person, who I must point out again, is just not that special.

Sometimes criticism really isn't about you, which, of course, is weird to hear when it appears to be directed at you. If they're attacking you or expressing disapproval about you not wanting to do something that would cause you to treat you without love, care, trust and respect, they're just showing and telling you who they are. Sometimes when people lash out, it's also about their own circumstances, especially when you realise that their reaction is so disproportionate to the matter at hand, it sure as hell isn't all about you.

People see things from their perspective. Many people when they express concern, opinions, and criticism about you or your life, are not thinking about you; they're either thinking about what they would be like under the same circumstances or are objecting to your actions inconveniencing them.

Sometimes criticism means, 'Please stop making it difficult for me to eff around with you and do things on my terms.'

Is there any truth in the criticism? What is it that you don't like about it? You don't have to accept a criticism in its entirety, but if you do recognise the truth, don't ignore it. That's how you have developed your fantasy ways in the first place. If what you don't like is how it was said or what you fear may be their next course of action, don't assume what is going to happen or put words in their mouths and ensure that anything you say or do next is based on reality, not what on you fear might happen.

It's OK to compromise by finding a solution that you can both live with, but this is very different to compromising yourself by sacrificing your boundaries and values. Make sure that you recognise the difference. Don't compromise in an effort to avoid conflict or criticism – you will wind up in an even worse situation than if you'd just faced them plus you'll be pissed off with you for selling yourself out. Quickly remedying a situation by rushing in with a misguided 'fix' means that it's a blind compromise based more on your fear and insecurity than it is on reality. Compromising shouldn't create a 'loss'.

You're not a child anymore, so make sure that you look at criticism and conflict through adult eyes and adjust your perspective. Now that you're an adult, how would you teach a child how to cope with not always hearing what they want to or dealing with conflict? Now pass some of that advice onto you.

Own your right to express disapproval and to deal with or even instigate conflict, and you will respect the right of people to express their disapproval or to instigate their own conflict. You don't have to like it and neither do they, but this is better than feeling victimised when you silence yourself or go against you.

LETTING GO OF ABANDONMENT

A few years ago, I accepted something that until that point I'd rejected, accentuating my fear of being abandoned: As a child, you can be abandoned, because you're not emotionally and physically equipped to take care of yourself in the world 'alone', but certainly as an adult, as long as I have a healthy relationship with myself which in turn paves the way for healthy relationships with others, I don't need to fear abandonment. This isn't to say that I wouldn't be devastated if I lost my partner but, even before my relationship, I had to become a fully functioning adult that forged relationships, not because I didn't want to be alone, or because they were perfect for avoiding my fear of abandonment, but because I was willing to healthily risk being available and vulnerable to experience intimacy and commitment. I also learned that I am more than capable of taking care of myself, emotionally, physically and spiritually.

If you feel that you have a pervasive fear of being abandoned, the first step is to actually get to know your fear and get professional support.

This will help you to learn to stand on your own two feet while having support with respectful boundaries to help you work through the issues that have stood in your way. Right now, you know your fear, but you don't *know* it, and instead of taking positive steps that would actually foster the independence and security that you need to reduce that fear, you're actually forging relationships that cater to and increase it.

You are anticipating what's next (possible abandonment) and fearing something that either isn't happening yet or isn't likely to happen (possible abandonment). That's a half-life at best. When you take steps in other areas of your life to ground yourself in reality, to build your self-esteem, and to emotionally and physically equip you to take care of you, the fear of abandonment will reduce.

Don't be afraid to ask for help – it is the choice between continuing to remain as you are in an uncomfortable comfort zone, or making a decision to seek help and help yourself, that will change the relationships you have and your experiences.

What you do need is to be realistic – can you commit to doing the work yourself, or do you feel that you need help? Bearing in mind that you've had a penchant for fantasy relationships, you may not be in the best position to judge this, and if you want to help and even speed up the process, seeking professional help and spending time in support groups will give you physical, real touch points in your life, that aside from helping you to deal with your fear of abandonment, also help you to remain in reality. This is critical.

I am amazed at how many people can invest money, time, and energy in everything else such as material goods or other people, and yet they have every excuse as to why they won't spend some money getting professional help that could literally change their lives. Don't be one of these people. You are worth the investment and, believe me, when you want to help yourself, you'll find a way.

Dealing with a fear of abandonment is not an overnight thing. It's not like you'd read this and wake up tomorrow and think, 'I'm alright, Jack!' That said, you can change how you feel about 'abandonment' and your personal security certainly in as little as a matter of months – I should know, I've done it myself.

When you say that you're afraid of abandonment, what you're really saying is, 'I'm afraid that they'll leave and I don't believe I'm capable of managing without them.' You're also saying, 'I can't cope with anyone else leaving,' which only confirms that your fear is very much tied to the unresolved primary experience that triggered your fear. The single biggest change in my life that changed how I felt about my own personal security was that I stopped looking for others to make my life secure. Experience has taught me that people make their own lives secure and expect to show up to a relationship where the other person has their own personal security.

Personal security based in another individual entity isn't personal; it's codependency.

I stopped looking for love in the wrong places, I accepted that a 'relationship' with a man with a girlfriend was causing me far more agony than if I'd accepted it was no-go, I stopped making a new me for each relationship and basing my identity on each partner, and I created security in my life and felt satisfied, and in fact happy, with what I'd created off my own steam. Nobody needed to validate me and the power to improve my life was put in my own hands. This fantasy where I could take someone who was unavailable with their own set of problems and make them the key to my life, brought me an incredible amount of pain and disappointment.

If you can have the power to create your own pain, you certainly have the power to create your own happiness and security – it's a redirection of energy.

Fearing abandonment can cause you to almost compulsively do things that, at best, leave you feeling embarrassed and, at worst, humiliated. What these things don't achieve is providing you with a sense of security or 'stopping' the 'abandonment'. This isn't because you are an 'abandon-able' person, but as explained in the chapter *Fear Of Abandonment*, you are seeking out relationships that, whether it's consciously or subconsciously, cater to your fears and put you in the position of realising the abandonment or at the very least reducing your self-esteem to rubble.

Unavailable relationships are 'great' for distracting you from where you're abandoning yourself.

As I'm not a doctor and this book, like all my books, is based on experience and observation, I'm obviously not going to offer you any medical advice – I'm going to assume that if you wanted something scientific, you either wouldn't be reading this book, or you would but you'd be either arranging some type of therapy, or using this as a stepping stone to delve deeper into more research on the subject. I haven't even done therapy myself, although I have many readers who have found it useful, so what I do want to share are some key things that I've learned that have reduced my fear of abandonment from being a heightened, pervasive fear, to being minimal.

Independence blows apart a fear of abandonment. People who find it difficult to recover themselves after the loss of a relationship, struggle because they haven't maintained their identity which is all tied up in someone who isn't around, or who, actually, was never truly around.

- Don't sack off your friends and family every time you meet someone new.
- Don't ever isolate yourself to maintain the status quo of an unhealthy partnering.
- Create hobbies and interests that are specific to you – they're done to enjoy, to broaden your horizons, and to form part of your social life, not to make you more attractive for a mate.
- Have a job, save some money, no matter how small, and learn how to take care of yourself emotionally and physically.
- Learn how to do things alone, not because you're preparing to be screwed over, but because it's good to learn how to enjoy your own company.
- Try new things. First stop meetup.com which has been tried by so many readers.
- Invest in professionals or experiences that enable you to discover more

about who you are and realise your strengths. Check with local support networks, your doctor's surgery, and hospital about support groups and even mini courses in your area that enable you to grow your confidence, learn new skills, or work through previous experiences.

It's a lot harder to be abandoned when you haven't abandoned yourself. Figure out who you are independently of partners, your family or your past, and work out what is important to you – your values. There is no faster way to abandon yourself, than to do things that detract from you by treating you, or allowing others to treat you without love, care, trust and respect, and not having boundaries, or living in line with your values.

If you don't have your back, guess what? Of course you're going to be afraid of people abandoning you because you expect others to do what you do to yourself.

Don't base your identity on your abandonment. I, like many of my readers have been The Girl Whose Daddy Abandoned Her. There's also The Girl Whose Daddy/Mama didn't give her enough emotional attention, The Girl Whose Parents Were Too Screwed Up/High To Raise Her Properly and The Girl Who Was Left By A Man Who She Thought Would Be Around Forever More. These identities are neither useful or flattering and keep you in a helpless, victim mode. These are experiences, not a seal burned into you that tells the world what your character and values are. There's more to you than your experience of abandonment. This doesn't change what happened but it doesn't have to define you – this is as good a time as any to find out who you are and you can choose differently.

Be in relationships where you are the only person and are treated and regarded as a priority not an afterthought. Married and attached men, men who breeze in with a few texts or calls and then vanish, men who promise to take care of you and then are nowhere to be seen, are not where it's at. Nobody, even someone who didn't arrive into a relationship with a fear of abandonment, would feel secure in this environment. Cut them loose.

Sounds so simple but it's amazing how many people neglect to recognise this – **if you struggle with abandonment anxiety, don't involve yourself with anyone that exacerbates it or quickly remove yourself out of any situation that exhibits signs of it.** Either use external evidence to support the decision to opt out, or use familiarity. If the situation feels familiar and you're actually behaving in similar ways, this is a code red alert – you're trying to evolve so familiarity is not on the cards here. It is easy to rationalise that if you were more this and that, that you wouldn't have the anxiety – that wouldn't change who they are. Remember that you are two separate identities. Which brings me neatly to...

If you continue to accommodate shitty behaviour in an effort to avoid abandonment, all you end up with is an increased sense of abandonment and the effects of being abused or taken advantage of. This removes your sense of personal security and increases your dependence – it's the nature of abuse. If you stop accommodating shitty behaviour, your personal security rises because you realise that you've got your back. Remember, it's your back to have. Other people who have it are a bonus, but until you have your back, nobody has it and there are people who will only be too happy to put their foot on it and turn it into a doormat.

Don't look for partners with an agenda of finding someone to take care of, finance you, and make your world right. Of course we all want love, care, trust, respect and a level of financial security in our relationships, but this is stuff that you should be doing for yourself anyway. If you neglect to do these things for yourself, well, of course anyone who comes along and talks a good game and throws out a few crumbs already looks great by comparison.

Don't treat people like they're the irreplaceable oxygen and power supply in your life. It screams desperation, making it difficult for you to believe you can survive on your own because the source of your misery is also the sole source of your happiness.

Stay you. Don't twist, turn, morph and adapt to accommodate what you think someone else wants and needs. This very quickly shifts into codependency, where, as a result of abandoning yourself and changing you to suit them, you feel like you're no longer a separate entity. You also then want to believe that you've gone to the trouble of doing things that go against your values or reject you as a person for a reason, and so will keep flogging at the relationship, while you continue losing yourself.

Avoid relying on those who have proved themselves to be unreliable to be there in a time of need. All this does is continue to build on an unhealthy foundation and create an opportunity for someone who isn't there for you, to yet again not be there for you. Stop setting them tests, stop looking to be the exception, and don't use times of need as a way of triggering decency out of someone who has a habit of screwing you over.

Start to practice self-control. If you have a habit of calling or texting to check up on someone, let's say ten times a day, it's time sit on the urge and gradually reduce it down. Drop one call for a couple of days, then drop two a day for a few days, then get to three and basically keep reducing each week until you get down to at least half of what you are doing. The reason why you should be getting in touch with someone shouldn't be based wholly and solely on satisfying your fear that they haven't run off with someone in the couple of hours since you last spoke. If you remember that trying to control another person and their agenda can be seen as abuse, and no doubt you don't even want to be associated with that, recognise that control or the illusion of it is not love. I love when Jennifer Hudson sings, 'I don't like... living under your spotlight', but instead of saying that if you treated them better you wouldn't have to worry, if you treated you better, you wouldn't have to worry because you'd choose better and have a grip on your own life.

Some relationships have to and should end. If you keep seeing your relationships not working out as abandonment, aside from each person having what is closer to a parental role in your life, you're too busy trying to hold onto them at all costs and make them fulfil what you feel is their obligation to take care of you and never leave, that you miss some very obvious reasons as to why the relationship isn't healthy and shouldn't be forced to continue.

Instead of chasing when you experience someone blowing hot and cold, register it as the code red that it is. Chasing someone who is flip-flapping actually increases a sense of rejection, not reduces it.

You don't have to keep reliving the pain of your abandonment if you take the steps to come to terms with what has happened. It doesn't mean that it is forgotten but it does remove the power it has over your present. Aside from professional help, Unsent Letters can be incredibly therapeutic, especially because you have an opportunity to forgive you so you can devote the rest of your life to loving you.

GETTING CONTROL UNDER CONTROL

I can tell you right now, that most of the angst that people experience around unhealthy relationships is about not being able to get inside the other person's head, to control their opinion, what they're thinking, and what they're intending, and the inability to influence and direct another person's behaviour by throwing your love, attention, sex, imagination and even texts at them. You're not about to be able to read people's minds or take over the controls, so it's you that has to get a grip on trying to control the uncontrollable. The funny thing is that when you align yourself around people who have similar values and are a reflection of a healthy relationship with yourself, while you still will never know every thought in their head or be able to control their actions, you have greater sense of trust, both in you and in them, which allows you to get on with exerting influence over your life.

Love is not about having the power to change or control someone. It's also not a power struggle so rather than vying to control a relationship that you feel has left you helpless, it's better to go and be in a relationship where you can accept and respect both you and them, that you're both copiloting.

I know it feels like everything is about you because you are you and it's your life, but not everything is about you. The only thing that is about

211

you is you and your actions. Everybody else's actions are about them. You're just not that powerful that you're making people be and do certain things. You're certainly not causing a radical change in personality – people be and do what they're already inclined to do. The world is not manoeuvring to your I'm Not Good Enough Record – people are far too caught up in themselves.

Learn how to trust you. There's no easier way to feel out of control than by placing all of your trust in others, and very little of it in yourself. You learn how to trust you by exercising your judgement through experience. This is how you learn to have confidence in yourself because you can trust you to look, listen, and act in your own best interests. It also means that even in the face of 'bad news', you're OK because at least you hear and see and know it's bad news and are acting upon it so it doesn't become something considerably bigger and unnecessary.

When you learn how to trust you, you learn to trust your capabilities in various circumstances. I, like many Fallback Girls, have told myself many times in the past that I couldn't handle something and then subsequently became obsessed with being in control of 'everything' to prevent me from having to deal with what I was afraid of. You're stronger than you give yourself credit for.

Perfection doesn't exist. There's no such thing as a perfect life or a flawless human. Trying to control 'everything' in an attempt to make things the way that you view as perfect, is far from 'perfect' behaviour. Many people spend their whole lives not appreciating themselves or their lives because of a goal of perfection. When you relax into yourself and your life and seek to feel good and happy instead of perfect, there is a whole life waiting for you to enjoy, including bouncing back when things don't always go how you'd like.

You do not need to get all of the details of your relationship 'right' or

look for ways to correct them through new encounters – let yourself and your experiences unfold. Let even your 'mistakes' unfold because you're too busy trying to correct along the way, often using your ego as a basis for your actions, before you truly see what insights you can gain from the experiences. If you keep trying to control everything, you just don't step back enough to have an objective view.

See the wood, instead of the trees. When you're busy trying to control other people's opinions or actions, or limiting yourself in limited relationships so that you don't have to stretch you emotionally, you miss the big picture – that this relationship isn't working for you, or that you aren't actually getting any genuine happiness and fulfilment out of these unproductive uses for your energy, or that your life is passing you by. Is it really worth devoting weeks, months or even years of your life trying to 'correct' a person's opinion or win back a relationship that is over for good, healthy reasons?

Pseudo control isn't control; getting behind the wheel of your life and driving it is. Being in control in your head is of shag all use to you – you need to be influencing and bringing about change in your own life, through your own actions.

Look at what you're trying to control in others – how could you create this in your own life? One example is that when you try to devote your energies to controlling the opinions of others, it's because you are exerting little control over the opinion of yourself – you're just letting your negative self talk run riot. Another is when you try to control another person's agenda and keep tabs on them because it feels like they're off creating their own life while you're stagnating. Stop tracking them, stop stagnating, start creating your own life. Watching over them isn't going to do it.

Remember that when you refuse to accept that the relationship is over or attempt to coerce them into doing things your way, you're attempting to control their agenda and possibly even bombarding them with attention. This will alienate you. Breakups are not a democratic decision and people have their own agendas, which means that they don't need your agreement to break up and you have to step back and get on with your own agenda, without them. In a mutual relationship, you have a joint agenda. Stop wrestling with this person for power – let them go.

Practice acceptance. I don't mean accept bullshit behaviour, but what I do mean is that it's to accept how things are, instead of rejecting it in favour of complaining about how you want things to be like how they used to be or how you believe they should be in the future. You cannot control the past and you certainly only have control over what you choose to do in your own future.

Accept that you cannot control others but you can control you. This is natural, normal and nothing to be ashamed of. It doesn't mean you're not good enough or that you're a failure or that you should have tried harder or whatever else you're telling yourself. There is no person on this planet that you can control other than you. When you recognise that you don't have this power, while your first instinct may be to feel helpless, what you need to give way to, is you not blaming yourself for other people's actions and not being able to do something that nobody other than abusers can do, which means that you can claim the power that's rightfully yours. Trying to control others does create a feeling of helplessness but every day you have to make a choice between being helpless by trying to control others you can't control, or being powerful by empowering you in your own life.

Nobody else should be directing or influencing your worth or your life other than you. This is the same for everyone else, so you need to get on with assuming responsibility for yourself and leave everyone else to do theirs.

HOW TO BE REAL

Right now, you've been engaging in a pattern of being unrealistic which in turn has led to 'relationships' that have too much imagination not enough reality, which in turn has opened you up to your hopes and expectations being unfulfilled and exacerbating your feelings about rejection. And round and round and round and round we go. In *Mr Unavailable and the Fallback Girl*, there's a whole section on breaking your pattern and other tools that you can use to start moving towards being available. As a Dreamer, there are some key habits that you can focus on turning into old habits by replacing them with new ones.

CUT THE BIG 5 OF BULLSHIT OUT OF YOUR LIFE

Assumptions. Basically stop deciding and accepting that something is true without sufficient proof. More importantly, while we're all allowed to make a few assumptions, they're only there as a baseline for you to evaluate a person or a situation based on the feedback of what has actually resulted. Re-assess and evaluate your assumptions and adjust to reflect reality to turn them into knowledge.

Rationalising. Stop trying to explain, justify and even excuse something with what you feel are plausible explanations which, of course, can end up crossing into denial. Your plausible explanations are not true, as exemplified by your fantasising. Using fantasy as a logical basis for a course of action is dangerous. This is how people remain stuck in abusive relationships.

Minimising. Playing down the truth of something, or its significance, to stop the unpleasant truth from disrupting your fantasy. This is how people wake up in abusive relationships.

Excuses. These are reasons given to justify an occurrence, fault or offence, but their primary objective is to lessen responsibility which in turn lets you overlook what you shouldn't. Behind every excuse is the real reason – even if you don't like it, heed it.

Denial. Refusing to admit the existence of something puts you in a complete fantasy and is incredibly dangerous. Accept the existence so that you can take action.

STICK TO THE FACTS. EYES WIDE OPEN, BRAIN SWITCHED ON.

Use eyes and ears to observe and avoid adding layers of imagination because it is the latter action that causes you to read far more into a situation than exists and/or to build sandcastles in the sky. It's all about being in the now for long enough as opposed to jumping out of the present into how you'd prefer things to be or planning out your future.

You need to build up a person, not start with an image of them that you then have to try to figure out how the hell to pull them apart and make them real. Imagine a Lego person – you start with one brick and you add more and more bricks until you get the full picture. Currently, you travel with your own readymade Lego person in your mind. You shouldn't be adding bricks until you have seen whatever you characteristics, qualities and values consistently demonstrated. As you build up the person through discovery, if a piece that you've added doesn't fit any longer because you've seen evidence that contradicts what you believed, take it out.

Anyone can be anything for a few weeks, or even a few months, but time shows you who someone truly is, as does reality, such as having to share your lives together and even overcoming conflict or difficult times. The honeymoon period and excitement is not an automatic precursor of what comes next.

Stop, look, listen, and watch. When you're serious about looking for a lasting relationship, you don't put the bulk of your energy into being swept along, writing emails and texts or having sex. You can like someone, have a good time and look for and learn information to back up your growing feelings. You also need to engage in experiences that enable you to spend time together and truly get to know one another. This cannot happen if you're at a distance or living from high to high.

Take your time. When people throw themselves into something in a hurry, they do it based on assumptions. This is difficult to do with a stranger who has their own agenda and who hasn't fully revealed themselves to you yet. It's a lot easier to hurry into something, when it's, for example, a work project. Even then, you'd hope that if you went into a project in a hurry and conflicts with your beliefs revealed themselves, that you'd be leaving enough room to adapt to these.

Stop putting so much energy into anticipating what's next so you can be in the present, which is where you can see how things truly are instead of fantasising about what you'd like to be next. This is particularly true in the early stages of a relationship where there just isn't enough time and experience to justify you leaping so far ahead.

Try meditation. Practising mindfulness ensures that you're spending the bulk of your time in your conscious. It can also help you home in on feelings that you're avoiding. There are plenty of books and websites out there, plus wherever you're based, it's highly likely that there is some form of local support in the form of classes. I highly recommend Headspace

217

(www.getsomeheadspace.com) who make meditation easy and accessible for everyone, with plenty of quick videos and tips, plus a handy iPhone and Android app that will even ping and remind you to be mindful for 10 minutes every few hours. If you're based in the UK, they also do inspiring seminars.

If you don't ever want to be in the position of questioning what was real and what was fake, accept NO illusions.

- Is it real?
- Can I touch it?
- Can I experience it in the real world?
- Does this person exist?
- Any 3rd party involvement?
- Any code amber I should be addressing or code red I should be opting out of?

Don't override any concerns – differentiate between fear and knowledge. Fear means something isn't happening yet, but knowledge means it is or has – make sure that you know the difference between the two, because knowledge but still focusing on being afraid of what you actually already know indicates that you are ignoring vital information that you should be processing and acting upon because you are afraid of the truth. The longer you ignore knowledge, is the greater the illusions, is the harder the fall.

COPILOT OR FLUSH – NO FLOATING AND COASTING

The only option that will reduce experiencing many of the things that you fear and avoid is to copilot mutual relationships. When you allow yourself to be swept along as a passenger, either throwing yourself into another person's agenda while sacking off your values, or going along with their agenda with a view to trying to push your own agenda at a later date, you set yourself up to build sandcastles in the sky by making a baseless and dangerous assumption that if you do tag along that there's a reward at the end of the yellow brick road. Copilot or flush. No letting anyone manage down your expectations and stick you on their terms, and no being helpless and jumping on whatever trainwreck relationship that comes along. Copilot or flush.

When you're in a mutual relationship, they're not just focused on what they can do and you're not just focused on what you can get from them. There's mutual love, care, trust, respect and you're genuine in your support of one another instead of having agendas. You'll also work together to resolve the conflicts that will arise so that you can find a mutually beneficial outcome – a solution you can both live with.

Resist the urge to overcompensate. As soon as you do, you very quickly see whether you're on a level footing with someone or whether they're riding on your coattails.

- Don't do things with a view to triggering decent behaviour – it's only telling you that you're not happy with their current behaviour.

- If you make a call, or send a text/email and haven't got a response yet, don't follow up with a flurry of contact, especially in the early months of your relationship. Aside from looking insecure when you do panic, by avoiding overcompensating, you'll see where you stand.

- **Slow your roll.** If you dive in head first because you're on a fantasy high, you're already overcompensating. Slow it right down so you can see your respective contributions objectively.

Absolutely no putting people on a pedestal. Stop talking and pumping them up! Stop believing that they're oh so special because they're 'important' or good looking, or intelligent or said something nice to you. They are an ordinary person and if you put them on a pedestal you create an automatic imbalance that creates too many expectations of the other party. If the pedestal isn't removed quickly, the relationship will fail anyway.

USE DATING AS A DISCOVERY PHASE

Here's how you currently work. You meet someone, your fantasy device is activated and whatever image you have in your mind at that point and whatever assumptions you're rolling with, that's about all the discovery that you seem to think you need to do. Dating is a discovery phase for you to find out the facts about a person.

- **Observe the person in action**, something that's not going to happen if most of your time is spent alone, or on the other end of a phone or computer.

- Your job during the discovery phase isn't to look for reasons to justify the image you have or any dodgy assumptions you've made; **your job during discovery is to start out with a fresh canvas and discover who they are.** You don't have to justify anything if you start out with your feet on the ground with your eyes and ears open.

- **Talk in real time.** Yeah, I'm sure you're going to learn about one another's pasts and yeah, I'm sure you're going to talk about the future, but how about you both talk about the present and spend enough time getting to know one another there before you start building sandcastles in the sky.

- Let them demonstrate themselves to you consistently in the present before you entertain plans and promises that have no foundation.

- **Don't assume you want to or must continue.** Evaluate whether what you have seen and experienced so far (in reality, of course) is what you want and need from someone whom you want to have a relationship with.

Ask questions and raise discussions even if it raises conflict or reveals information you'd rather not know but need to. Remember that questions left unanswered and discussions left undiscussed create assumptions. There's a whole section on this in *Mr Unavailable and the Fallback Girl* but after reading many a tale of fantasy involvements, here are key questions that will prove very handy:

1) **Are you single?** Other variations: Are you involved with anyone else at the moment? Are you married or attached?

2) **What did you mean by that?** Six simple words that can take angst drama from a 10 to about a 5. When someone says something that leaves you perplexed, hurt, or whatever, ask. Better still, say, 'What did you mean when you said _____?' and repeat what they said.

3) **When will I be seeing you next?** Or When shall we get together next? A vague response or even no response tells you all you need to know. If it's not in the next 7 days and there really isn't a genuine reason such as they're in a coma, or they're out of town this week, then don't bother investing because big gaps give too much time for idle minds. If you're too afraid to ask, but you don't end up seeing them each week, you have your answer anyway.

4) Can you give me a call this evening (or whenever) and let's catch up then? This will quickly separate the wheat from the texting chaff.

5) **How about we arrange to meet?** If after reading this, you still find yourself in a long distance thing, you need to close the first meeting within 4-6 weeks of communicating and then follow through with an actual meeting. If after reading this book, you still find yourself chatting with some stranger that you met on a dating site for a few weeks, you need to nip it in the bud immediately. If you haven't met within a week or two and you both live in the same town/city, it's time to flush. For more on this, see my *Tips For Virtuals* chapter.

Slow. Your. Roll. No more Fast Forwarding! From thinking and feeling things that outpace the true nature of the relationship, to actually believing that it's credible for someone you hardly know to be making huge declarations after a fortnight or for you to be planning to run off into the sunset, it's time to get off the rollercoaster. Even if it means you need to sit on your hands, knit, take up a sport, go for a walk, jump on the treadmill (great for focusing busy minds as well as working your body), you are no longer allowed to speed date yourself. No good will come of it. Your idea of slow and possibly even 'boring' is actually reality – when you spend enough time there, you'll come to enjoy it because you know what? Beyond the short-term, you're not actually enjoying your fantasy existence very much.

Increase the amount of time it takes for you to feel emotionally attached and heavily invested. There are levels of attachment and investment. Being greatly attached to the idea of someone in spite of not actually knowing them, is disproportionate and suggests that you have no 'levels'. Accept that all dating and relationship interactions, no matter how small, have a time and energy investment, but this doesn't mean that ipso facto, you must get heavily emotionally attached to all interactions or that you must get a 'return' on your investment.

- **Start out with being curious/liking someone,** then move to liking/fancying them, then move to fancying them a lot, then give the relationship a chance to progress through the early months, particularly the honeymoon phase, and let your feelings grow over time based on real interaction and a healthy foundation, which in time may grow to love.

- **Don't assume that because you like someone that you're going to love them.** You're not telepathic – if you are, you should be putting your skills to good use. There's quite a lot that needs to happen between like and love – make sure that you experience plenty in reality before you make the switch.

- **Over time, your emotional attachment will healthily increase.** That said, if you each maintain your respective identities, you will have interdependence (which is healthy dependence) as opposed to codependence, which is where you have an unhealthy attachment to someone.

- **Check your level settings.** Dreamers seem to have three settings. 'Off' 'Curious/like' 'Love' (read: heavily emotionally attached). Sometimes you go from 'off' to a brief touch on 'curious' to 'love' very quickly. You need to spend more time in the curious/like phase and use the discovery phase of dating to question the curiosity and the liking, and then develop it based on real interaction.

- Certainly if it's in under 2-4 weeks, you are in the lust stage. Remind yourself of this to bring you back to base.

- There's a difference between liking someone a lot and being attached to the idea of not experiencing another rejection, which really has nothing whatsoever to do with actually liking the person a lot or being positively emotionally attached.

- If you do feel very attached and invested and you've known them for a short period of time or haven't actually seen them very often (minimum once a week and increasing over the first three months), this is actually your mind's way of giving you a red flag warning that you need to reground yourself.

Recognise and accept incompatibility. Even if you feel wildly attracted, if there is a conflict in values which ultimately govern how you each want to live and conduct yourselves, you are incompatible.

No matter how much you fantasise your way over this 'hurdle', a difference in core values is actually a dead end telling you to turn around and walk away.

Be honest even when it's uncomfortable. Honesty comes packaged up with respect – respect of yourself, other people, and the truth. Don't engage in selective honesty.

TIPS FOR ESCAPISTS

Watch Out For These Hotspots!

Fantasising about, or having an affair with a colleague.

The Returning Childhood Sweetheart that's looked you up while they're going through a 'rough patch' or divorce.

Dating sites specifically for people who are in relationships.

The affair with your friend's husband/partner or someone in your social circle who is also escaping their own problems which you may well be aware of.

Starting to privately communicate with a forum member/blog owner.

Try meditation. This is useful for all Dreamers but you should find it useful as you spend too much time escaping your own life.

Look at what it is that you're seeking from your fantasy relationship – fun, feeling attractive, attention, calm etc – and then look at where you can create that in your life in a way that respects both you and your current relationship and ultimately empowers you. It's perfectly OK to have needs but you're exacerbating your problems by checking out. Many Escapists feel crowded out of their own lives by the challenges of having a family and seek excitement to reconnect with The Time Before Kids and others are in a long marriage/relationship with someone they like, but that they've stopped feeling like their needs are being met.

Practice gratitude. I know so many people, both through my work and personally, who are taking the time to write down something that they're thankful for each day. Just considering one thing can make a difference, but you can often find several. It is a way of showing appreciation for your life and the lessons that you learn through your experiences. What do you have? We spend far too much time thinking about what we don't have – what do you have, right here, right now? Who has shown or told you who they are today? What have you learned about yourself through the mirror of other's actions or how you've reacted to an experience? What's the flipside of something that's worried or angered you today? What do you have to be thankful for? Until you begin to experience gratitude for the life you have, you cannot expect more experiences and opportunities to come along that you don't appreciate anyway because you're too busy seeing your life as not being 'enough'.

Couples counselling. If you haven't given up entirely on your relationship it's time to put in a renewed, concerted and consistent effort into the relationship. To save it from being a conversation that doesn't turn into action, make it clear that this is needed by both of you in order to move forward realistically.

Therapy. If you have various issues that you need to address or are finding that your partner is unwilling to go to counselling, go ahead and see a professional. Ensure that you engage someone that works with you to problem solve as opposed to lying there for years on end talking. If there are issues from your childhood that affect your ability to emotionally engage today, invest some time, energy, and yes, money, to address these.

Put together a list of your concerns or issues with your current relationship. This is a bit of an airing out. Don't censor yourself – be as bitchy and frustrated as you like with your list and pour out everything that's niggling at you, which is pretty cathartic in itself. Then re-look at your list and see where you can organise it into the core issues, and others that are gripes. Then look at what you can address on the list within you – you'd be amazed at how many people's lists of gripes contain things that they themselves are doing or are actually in a position to do something about.

Refocus on the neglected areas of your life. In every Escapist's life are neglected zones that have been shrouded in cotton wool by the fantasising. Whatever these are, avoiding them isn't the solution – confronting these areas and having a plan of action is. Brainstorm solutions and ensure that anything you come up with, has you as the driver so that you can be in control of making your life better.

Feelings Diary. Invaluable for tracking how you feel and your responses to it, as an Escapist you can get a sense of what is happening in your day that's pushing your check out reflex. You will quickly see if it's boredom, frustration, anger and when you see the pattern, you can look at constructive ways to deal with these issues so that you change the meaning and the outcomes that you apply when these issues arise.

Keep a What I've Done Today Task list. Yes you could write a todo list, but what I want you to do each day is write a list of what you've accomplished out of your day, no matter how small it is. This not only gets you to see how much of your day may be spent going through the motions and even dragging out one thing, but it causes you to refocus and make your days more conscious and productive.

Goals list. Dreamers love to dream and Escapists love to have a dream but feel frustrated about it not happening and mentally check out. Put together a list of your short-, medium- and long-term goals – pour everything into it and add to it as things come to you. Start knocking the short-term things off the list and considering what the next actions are with your longer term goals. What can you do to align your life with things that you aspire to be and do? Think about these and write them down. Goals lists are very empowering and help you to refocus your energy on your life. They reorganise your mind and even if you don't consult it very often, they can be enough to give you the kick up the pants you need.

Cut off all exes. If you insist that some are friends, ensure that there is absolutely no inappropriateness – ego stroking, you offloading your problems with your current partner on them. If your partner is unaware of the friendship, let it go. Painful as it will be, you can't continue using exes to distract you from your responsibilities – you and your relationship.

Write out your expectations. What do you expect from you, others, life, your relationship? Sometimes it's good to put it all out there so you can get a sense of what lies beneath. Then it's time to evaluate whether it's realistic. Two things that can quickly gauge this. 1) Write Dear [insert your name] at the top of the sheet and at the bottom write from/love [insert, for example your partner's name]. Now read it back. Does it sound realistic? Does it sound judgmental? OTT? How do you feel? 2) Of the things that you expect from others and life, how many of these do you embody right now? Make sure you have evidence to back up your claims. Look at where you can stand to re-evaluate your positions on these things. If any of these expectations involve a partner and haven't been communicated, you need to – people don't find out what you want by osmosis, tension or hinting.

Address your mode of staying and complaining. Griping is a comfort zone but you can't have it both ways. Either stay for the right reasons and find a resolution that you can both live with that respects both of you, or go. People who stay and complain do so because it gives an impression of busyness when actually, it's an avoidance of action. Complaining suggests that it's all on everything and everyone else – you are the driver of your own life. If you don't like how things are, do something about it.

TIPS FOR CRUSHERS

Watch Out For These Hotspots!

After a breakup, or what you perceive as a rejection, is when you're most likely to crush.

Bereavements can have you seeking solace and distraction with your imagination.

The person who seems to be very kind and patient with you – if you're used to a diet of crumbs, you are highly likely to read more into their actions.

A friend's partner who isn't being treated that well by them – you may imagine you could love them better.

Work is a major crush zone especially if you spend lots of time with one colleague.

Someone that you see regularly – church, gym, yoga, supermarket, local cop, the train, park, playground. You're likely to attach meaning to seeing and speaking to them, especially if there appears to be a frisson that's not acted upon.

Familiarity is your friend. If you respond to an attraction with your usual crushing behaviour, it's a red flag warning telling you to wake up and avoid your pattern.

Stop romanticising them. You may think you're not, but you are, otherwise you wouldn't be having this crush. It's hard to hear, but aside from the obvious that they're not perfect, they're also not the person for you. Take them off their pedestal and see them realistically, flaws and all instead of acting like they're perfect and you're the flaw preventing the possibility of a relationship.

Make them real. There's nothing like a good honest picture to give you a reality check on someone. Get a piece of paper and create a picture of them. Who are they? What is it that you like about them? Is everything that you like true and factual, or is any of it assumed or even exaggerated? As they're a real person, give them some habits and some pet peeves – what are their bad points? What irritates you? Have they got issues that prevent you from taking this beyond a crush? Are you idolising them like a cheerleader or fan? Remember that these are not the basis of a proper relationship – much like public relations is about communicating positive messages about products and services even though not all products and services that use PR are actually as great as they're made out to be, blowing smoke up someone's bum and putting them on a pedestal does the same thing.

No more excuses. I have heard every bullshit reason under the planet of why the object of a person's affections hasn't noticed them or isn't reciprocating. Enough. It's not because they're shy, the busiest person on the planet, scared of their feelings or whatever – these are bullshit reasons for disinterest and/or them being unavailable. Shy people make moves and communicate their interest, everyone is busy and plenty of people are scared of their feelings but more scared of missing out. The people who stay scared are unavailable anyway.

Don't project your reasoning and excuses onto them either. You may reason that you're scared or you're shy, but guess what? If you were really that interested, you'd make your interest clear. If off the back of this, they make no move or reciprocate with some feeble unavailable effort, it's time to flush. Remember crushing on someone that you know is a long shot and who in fact is highly likely to stay a nothing relationship, is avoidance, not interest.

Feelings Diary. Identify what it is that you're trying to avoid, whether it's uncomfortable feelings, or having to deal with a particular situation, such as moving your life forward after a breakup. Keep a record of what has happened on days where your feelings for them intensify and keep a note of when and why you hit despair – here amongst your feelings which you're being hijacked by, lies the truth. Find it. Also learn to recognise the signs that you have a crush developing – this gives you an opportunity to reground yourself and invest your energy into more productive uses.

No dwelling. Instead of running with the thought when it pops into your head, arrest the thought and replace it with something else. It's like pulling over for a moment when you fall asleep at the wheel. Collect your thoughts and replace it with positive thoughts about you or positive productive uses of your energy such as plans you're making to follow through on, stuff you need to do that day. Put together a goto list of subjects (3-5 are good) and pick one each time your mind wanders. Mine were my health, specifically what I needed to do that day to boost my immune system, something I was planning to purchase, something I was planning to eat, reminding myself of exactly why the outcome of us not being together was a good thing, and correcting anything harsh that I'd said about myself. Sometimes I'd say, 'You're better than selling yourself short,' which was an empowering kick up the bum to keep pushing for better.

Set a time limit for 'closing time'. In sales they refer to closing the deal. While I appreciate that we are not always in the position to act immediately or very quickly upon feelings, as you have a habit of being a Crusher and it's affecting your emotional availability, you need to set a time limit. One to two months max and I'm being generous. How much time have you got left to squander? Be a closer. Before you object, this is not the same as being an aggressive terrier. Ask them out – if you are direct instead of ambiguous, you will either get a direct answer or if you get an ambiguous response, you know that you need to back off and accept that they're not interested. Of course you can flirt and drop hints, but do allow for the fact that everyone's perception of flirting and dropping hints is subjective plus it's likely to miss the message spot. "Would you like to go for a drink/bite to eat on X day?"

Let go of the hope. Look, I know it's hard to face disappointment but when you do, you are free to be available for someone who will reciprocate and pursue you. Stop waiting around for them to notice you – this can become a very demeaning activity, especially if you have to watch them play out their relationship with someone else. This also includes not trying to orchestrate this relationship – if you have to drag the horse to water to make it drink, it isn't going to feel naturally inclined or happy about drinking from that water in the future. Do ya catch my drift? You coerce a man into noticing you, you'll have to coerce him into everything else as well – you'll never feel secure in the relationship.

Get on with your own life. My friend's brother fancied a woman for four years before they finally got together. She was with someone else. Rather than put his life at a standstill, he didn't wait around for her and he accepted that much as he liked her, she didn't fancy him right now and he had to let her go. They crossed paths again and both of them were single – he seized the moment, asked her out and they're now married three years on.

Remember, everyone has crushes from time to time but they become unhealthy when they take over your life and prevent you from engaging in your present or affect your emotional availability. You can fancy someone without your life coming to an end and passing you by!

If you have a crush and spend a lot of the time mentally berating or even punishing yourself, this is not a healthy interest or activity. Feeling attracted to someone, no matter the outcome, should be something that makes you feel good, not a torture device. If you are running you down, it is time to focus on building your self-esteem.

Self-esteem is the difference between a long-standing crush, a blip or a conversion into a date. Why can't you act upon your feelings? Yes, asking them out runs the risk of 'rejection', but actually, it allows you to know where you stand, grieve the loss of hope, put things into perspective and move onto someone else. Equally, they could respond with yes. What you have to accept though, is even if they do reciprocate initial interest, you still have to go through the discovery phase and it doesn't mean you're destined to be together forever and ever. Accept that if they haven't asked you out, that they're not interested and it's their loss. Your whole identity doesn't rest upon someone who even if they have some level of interest, they're not acting upon it.

Attend grief counselling for your previous breakup(s). Are you over a previous breakup? Or have you tried to bury your feelings of hurt in a new purpose in the form of a crush? Are you feeling traumatised by the end of your relationship or marriage? Do you feel powerless? Has the breakup resurrected old hurts and childhood wounds? Have you made a judgement about you? Have you experienced a bereavement that this crush has provided a distraction from your grief? Grief counselling, bereavement or not, can be incredibly nurturing and empowering to help you come to terms with your losses and move forward. Locally, there are likely to be grief and even breakup support groups – look them up and go.

Take some personal development classes to help you build your confidence. This is a key ingredient in self-esteem, helping you to assert yourself, but to also have confidence in your abilities and to engage in positive self-talk. Before you start with the objections about money and time, at the very least buy a book and remember that you shouldn't really be complaining about investing in you – you're a sure bet as opposed to your long-shot guy.

Group activities are also good for building confidence and learning how to engage with people. Can't say this enough – get thee to meetup.com. I have very introverted friends who have blossomed since they've faced their fears and learned how not to run from running the risk of getting to know people and experiencing 'rejection'.

Get other areas of your life positively under your control – friends, family, work, health, finances etc. You will find that when you're in the driving seat of your life, you will not need to engage in pseudo control fawning over a crush.

Round out your life to reduce the sense of loneliness. I'd feel lonely if most of my time was devoted to idolising someone. They'll be a lot less interesting when you have fulfilling relationships and experiences in your life, including a more caring relationship with yourself. Get some hobbies and some interests. No I'm not suggesting that doing group activities or learning how to wrestle or whatever is a substitute for a loving, romantic relationship, but without having a rounded life, what you seek out of a romantic relationship is very distorted. Nobody wants to come along and be your whole life (unless they're like the man in *Sleeping With The Enemy*), so make your own life anyway.

If you sleep with the object of your affections and nothing happens, or they try to turn you into a booty call, back away. Fast. You're free to ask what the story is but let's be real – it doesn't take a genius to add two and two together and make four. Someone who is genuinely interested in you, would not back away and then try to downgrade you to an unpaid hooker. If nothing happens, you know that they're unavailable. At least you know where you stand now. Do not blame you for sleeping with them – it takes two to tango and you both have on big people's pants. You could have not slept with them and still ended up with the same outcome or be waiting around to have the same outcome at a later date. Let it be. They're just not *that* special.

If you ask what is going on and you get back that they're not interested or not ready for a relationship, accept it. They're unavailable and they're definitely not the one for you. Do not try to convince them and definitely don't switch back to crushing. Flush and grieve, flush and grieve.

Stop talking about their possible or lack of interest with friends, family, and colleagues, especially those who use conjecture and their gossipy ways to keep stoking the crush fire. They don't know and they shouldn't be pushing you to keep hanging around for someone who is not stepping up. Stop listening to their excuses. Say, 'I appreciate your concern, but this entire experience has had quite an effect on me and I no longer want to put my life on hold. I need to turn my attentions to myself and save my affections for someone who will reciprocate and act upon them.'

What qualities do you admire in the object of your crush? Find these within yourself. You don't need to get with somebody in order to be the things that you either already are or that you aspire to be.

If you only want to remain at a distance, accept that you're not *that* serious or that interested.

TIPS FOR VIRTUALS

Watch Out For These Hotspots!

Returning Childhood Sweetheart looking you up on Facebook, LinkedIn etc.
Reminiscing about old times with exes, which turn to sexts…
Texting someone you're interested in for months but never actually having a date.
Fresh out of a long-term marriage or relationship and 'new' to all of this virtual malarkey.
Looking for attention to avoid that pesky divorce.
A 'friend' from church or work, romancing you with words and big promises.

The amount of time between meeting someone online and meeting face to face should be short. The longer it is, the greater the fantasy. If you met someone in a face to face situation, you'd hopefully exchange numbers and agree to meet, because the exchange of numbers is on the basis that the person has expressed an interest in asking you out. All they have to do is ask and set a time and a date – simple. There is no need to go through this pre-vetting process by having long drawn out and misleading conversations via text, email, and even phone, without setting the date. You're not a hotline for stroking the ego of strangers. Dating is a discovery phase – use dates to discover before you invest into having these lazy communications with someone you hardly know. Shortening this time period will save you a hell of a lot of pain and illusions.

It's time for a lazy communication diet. You'd be amazed at how quickly you'll see how things really are when you opt to pick up the phone instead of texting or emailing, or opt to meet up instead of spending your days chatting.

Take at least a 3-6 month break from dating sites and don't go back until you're ready to have hide of rhino and be the Columbo in your life. If you have an extensive history of virtual relationships, I'd take a year's break. Delete your profiles so that you don't feel tempted to reconnect with those who track you down or to collect attention.

If texting, email, IM, and dating sites didn't exist, and it was, for example, 1998, what would you do in the same situation?

Accept that texts, emails etc are not the bread and butter of a relationship that lacks regular and increasing human interaction; they're the crumbs. In an otherwise genuinely effort-filled relationship, these means of communication are fine, but otherwise, they are a deluding and unproductive use of your time that stunts communication.

If you're not touching them more than you're having lazy communication with them, this is not the relationship you think it is.

Stop being so words focused – if you haven't got actions and relationship to match, you've got nothing but words and hot air.

If you are transitioning from a breakup, divorce etc, deal with this first. Stop using these involvements as a distraction. Texts etc are not going to get you over your breakup or provide you with the better relationship that you deserve.

If it hasn't progressed into a face to face, bonafide relationship after a month of this contact, cut it off. It won't be over because you forced a meeting; it'll be over because it was dependent on not meeting and you were both passing time.

No sexts, no arguing, and no discussions via text and email. People who are in a relationship don't have to rely on sexting to have a sexual relationship... It is completely inappropriate and quite passive aggressive to argue or attempt to have a meaningful discussion via text or email – face to face or voice to voice. If you want to clarify points post discussion or argument by text/email, that's one thing, but the truth is that mature, available adults don't use these means to have meaningful discussions about meaningful relationships. You must learn to communicate on a level with people and face your fear of conflict and rejection.

No long-distance relationships. 1-3 hours travelling is doable as long as you have the means to regularly make the journey. Some people are not cut out for long-distance relationships – Dreamers fit that bill. The lack of face to face interaction and the distortion caused by it being long distance, which adds a tension that wouldn't exist otherwise, is too dangerous for you. If the distance becomes too much and you spend more time thinking about the relationship than living it, let it go.

Be careful of being with people who spend a lot of their time travelling. Certainly in the early months, this is a vulnerable hotspot for you and leaves you too wide open. You need to be with someone who you can see regularly both during the week and at the weekends. This isn't to say that people who go away are unavailable – this is about you. Until you're in the position of being real and fully accountable, it is dangerous to have relationships that appear to give you an excuse to have too much alone time with your imagination and a legitimate reason to engage in crumb communication.

Accept that sex with primarily virtual contact isn't a relationship; it's a booty call with some window dressing.

Don't create new 'rules' to justify the lazy communication. Most Dreamers, especially Virtuals, have come up with all sorts of justifications for their behaviour based around modern dating. If you think that people are forging long-term relationships, getting married, having children, building lives together, by spending most of their time emailing, texting, IMing and waiting around, think again. Nothing has changed – in order to create a mutually fulfilling relationship with love, care, trust, respect and shared values, that has progression, consistency, commitment, balance and intimacy, you both need to be in the real world, seeing each other regularly and putting in genuine physical and emotional effort that matches your words. It does not matter that texting, dating sites, Facebook or whatever exist – it's only someone who wasn't intending to commit and has found new means to make it easier to make a big deal out of crumbs, that will rely on these means.

If you feel like you want to keep a safe distance, you probably shouldn't be involved. You're going to get to know someone by getting up close.

Respect your current relationship and, no matter how innocuous you think it is, don't entertain inappropriate interactions with people outside of your relationship. If you couldn't show your communications to your partner and they, in fact, have no knowledge of the person's existence, it is inappropriate.

Sort your problems out. Every person who is in a virtual relationship has problems that instead of solving, they avoid by seeking attention and making a big deal out of crumbs. This is how you end up with bigger problems than what you started out with. Sometimes we do need a distraction in order to gain perspective so that we can approach a problem with renewed vigour and focus; having a virtual relationship is not a means of doing this.

Bade farewell to your exes, especially the ones from long ago. Unless they add genuine, positive, out in the open and respectful value to your life, cut 'em off. This will mean grieving the loss of them, but you'd be surprised at how short this will be when you can grab back the power for your life and you realise that you're letting go of the best thing you never had so you can focus on experiencing the best thing that you can have in your future.

The ex from long ago that screwed you over, married someone else when you think you were so much better – let them go. They have made their choice and they're really not that special. Stop waiting around on the off chance that they might call you up after they've seen the light or tap you up for the role of the Other Woman. Stop stroking their ego, sending nude shots, or waiting around for them to send you dumb texts about the weather or your shared favourite sports team. It's all bullshit – you're better than this and you need to recognise that by allowing yourself to be a virtual emotional airbag, you're pumping up their ego and giving them an emotional exit that prevents them from facing their own problems in the real world. You are better than being a decoy.

If you are sleeping with several people at a time, or having sexual liaisons via text, IM, Skype etc with more than one person, or would be afraid to say how many people you are sleeping with each week/month, it is time to see a professional. That and please do ensure that you get your sexual health checked.

If you feel dependent on sending and receiving texts, emails, calls etc from someone who you're not actually having a relationship with, even if you think you are, seek help and support from organisations like CoDA (Co-dependents Anonymous). If you are a child of an addict, support groups like ACA (Adult Children of Alcoholics) or Al-Anon or similar groups can be incredibly useful during this time.

TIPS FOR TABBERS

Watch Out For These Hotspots!

The Future Faker who has abruptly left or disappeared.
The ex who has moved on to someone else very quickly.
The ex who won't return your calls or agree to debrief with you.
The dates with someone you met online that didn't work out that you thought would.
The ex who said something malicious, possibly in the heat of an argument that has left you stinging with rejection.

What are you afraid of? Try to elevator pitch it into a 30 second or less sentence or two. I'm afraid that if I don't know what he's doing all of the time that _____ is going to happen or that it will mean that I'm _____ which will mean _____. For example:

- I'm afraid that if I don't know what he's doing all of the time that it will mean that it's over between us which means that I will have to face my own life.

- I'm afraid that if I don't know what's happening in his life that someone else will have the opportunity to get away with hurting me which will make me look like I'm unworthy.

- I'm afraid that if I don't keep an eye that I will be made to look stupid and if I know what he's doing and saying, I can try and do something to change people's minds about me or change his.

Now take control of this fear and grab back your power. Is there a more rational view you could take of this thought? Are you being all or nothing, like you're only great if you're with him or crap otherwise? What is going to cost you more? Engaging in behaviour that treats you without love and adds to your pain or facing your fear? Take the power back.

If you're considering harming yourself or harming them, it's time to admit that you need help. There's nothing wrong with this and it can actually be quite liberating. Don't let the first time people recognise that you really need help be when it's too late or when you've taken revenge. Grief counselling can help you to process your anger, plus with the support of your doctor and other health professionals, you can nip this in the bud before the unexpressed anger that's turning to depression ends up having far reaching consequences for your emotional health and your life. You can recover from this.

This is a toughie, but no breaking and entering, calling up their work, making up false health issues, or trying to make them contact you by saying that you'll harm yourself. All of these behaviours indicate that you've reached a low point with this involvement and are trapped in your feelings. In an attempt to stem the rejection, you're doing anything and everything. One day you will look back on this time and have a slight cringe but be thankful that it's well behind you – make that day come faster by stopping now and going No Contact and getting any additional help that you need. There's more information on No Contact in my books *Mr Unavailable and the Fallback Girl* and *The No Contact Rule*.

Don't ignore your feelings of loss. Accept that the relationship is over and mourn the loss of it. Validate your feelings, not by stalking them, but letting the hurt come out. If that means that you weep, wail, rage, and feel tormented in the short-term, so be it – this is normal. It becomes not so normal when you deny these feelings or you experience them and pour fat on the fire by also being blindly angry with yourself. You have lost something – accept this so that you can start to make gains. CoDA, therapy and breakup support groups are wonderful – you realise you're not alone and there is life after the ex.

Consider the legal ramifications or even potential social consequences. List them. Imagine if you were found out – now what do you do to avoid this? The answer isn't to be more covert in your activities; it's to not put yourself at risk in the first place. You might think you have nothing to lose, but so does everyone who doesn't value something until they lose it and realise that they do.

Do a clean sweep for all forms of communication especially on the social networking side.

- **De-friend or hide on Facebook.** If you hide but then still keep looking, de-friend. It's better that you do it, than they do it. It will take a lot more effort to re-friend. Block so that they can't view you and you can't view them. Stop the torment.

- **De-friend mutual friends that aren't really friends.** If you are friends, hide their updates if they're in active contact with your ex. Any people that you do remain friends with, you must have a do not discuss or share policy – that means you cannot ask about your ex and they can't be telling you information about them. Also request that they don't share any information about you no matter how innocuous, with your ex and, if they do, de-friend.

- **Block or mute on Twitter.** Some apps allow you to mute someone's profile so that you don't see their updates. If you're not friends, unfollow and block. They can't see you (when logged in) and you can't see them.

- **Either block their email or create a filter** that prevents any emails from them from making it to your inbox.

- **If you have been logging into their email, stop immediately.** This is a criminal offence no matter where you are based and a serious violation of their privacy.

- **Delete your dating profile on sites that you're both on** and close your account so that it doesn't send you updates about your ex.

- Any and all forms of social network that allow you to have even the most meagre of windows into someone's life, need to be blocked or even removed. This may even include LinkedIn. If you need this for business, cut the tabbing and be professional.

- Don't de-friend or block and then re-friend and unblock and then block etc again – they may get notifications of these activities and you'll be stirring the pot.

- Only maintain social networks that add value to your life. If you feel it is too great a move to for instance, delete your Facebook account, it's time to find a more productive use of your time than tracking your ex.

- Delete apps and bookmarks off your phone so that you have to make a bit more effort to look them up.

- Use apps like Freedom on the Mac which can shut down access to your browser for most of the day. Not only is this great for focusing on work, but it's great for breaking temptation.

I guarantee you that if you were able to peek into the lives of your friends and colleagues, you would find that you're not the only person who has tried to cling on to whatever they can of an ex by compulsively looking them up. You're not unique and, in fact, the likes of Facebook are partially built on the premise of keeping in touch and noseying about in people's lives – you've just gone a bit too far and need to rein it in.

Take a social networking break. The amount of messages I get from readers who take the time to let me know that they're going to have a clean break from Facebook, Twitter etc for a month or few to get some perspective is increasing. If you've ever lost your phone for a few days and been incommunicado, after the initial panic, it's actually very freeing.

Limit your time. Even for me who doesn't keep tabs on people, I have to limit the amount of time I spend on distraction sites like Facebook, Twitter etc because they are a time suck. Once you've had a break, spend 5-10 minutes max and set a timer because from personal experience, hours can slip by just chatting shit and surfing about being a nosey parker.

Reduce the visits on a sliding scale. However many times that you visit a profile each day or whatever it is that you're doing, reduce it by half immediately and keep reducing by the same amount each week and phase out your visits. You do not need to satisfy your curiosity several times a day – this is torture. Don't expect immediate change in how you feel, if anything you will feel worse (temporarily) before you feel better. Let the process do its work – as the days and eventually weeks go by, you will suddenly realise that you're free.

Agree a time of the day that you get your 'one peek' and stick to it. This creates structure and accountability while you're phasing out your activities.

That said, if you have been doing anything illegal or that if the other party knew about it, they could get a restraining order out against you, you must cut off all forms immediately. It may seem harsh, but if you don't, you will use what feel like legitimate means to perpetuate the same behaviour.

Have a plan of action. Fill the space left by the end of the relationship – filling it with activity devoted to keeping track of them will only create a bigger void.

- Schedule a busy couple of weeks for yourself. Print out a calendar of the next fortnight and schedule the hell out of yourself.
- Tell 1 or 2 trusted people that for the sake of you cutting this off once and for all, that you're not allowed to attempt to contact your ex, or to keep checking your phone.

- Have a friend that you can call up when you feel tempted.

- Come up with a list of 5-10 things that you can do immediately to focus your attention elsewhere and replace your tabbing with productivity. Get on the treadmill, go out for a walk, declutter a cupboard or drawer (you'll have the whole house done eventually!), head down to the shelter to volunteer, bake, write, yoga, meditation etc.

- Whenever you go out anywhere, put your phone away from the moment you arrive until you leave, unless you have kids.

Feelings Diary. Tracking how you're feeling from day to day and where your angst and desire to control is coming from, can help you to gain perspective and control of your life. When you wake up, how do you feel? When you go to sleep, how do you feel? Right before you went on to Facebook or checked whatever, what were you thinking about? What did you believe that a specific action, such as checking up on them would achieve? What does knowing what they're doing tell you about you? How do you feel? At those times when you do feel in control (excluding keeping tabs on your ex), what is happening and what are you doing? How can you do more of this?

Assess the control you have over other areas of your life – what are you neglecting? Identify what your Tabber actions are distracting you from? What other things are challenging you in your life? What would you like to improve? Look into how. I've heard from a number of Tabbers who had experienced a loss of employment or a bereavement that in an effort to distract themselves, they'd focused on the ex to gain back the control. These situations are never easy and it's understandable to feel hurt and want to run from it at times, but doing what you're doing isn't going to get you a job, or bring back the person who you've lost, or whatever it is that you feel out of control about.

Or what is that you really want to have control over? It's not the person so figure out where you're really stuck. It was only very recently that I recognised that I became obsessed with trying to win over my ex with the girlfriend, because I felt out of control of my illness which was scary and made me want to avoid it, and because the ex before him had exerted so much control, it was also like trying to make up for lost time and a fight to gain the power. I knew I was ill, I just didn't want to face it. Most people who find a lump in their body would go to the doctor; I started an affair. When I faced my health and stopped waiting for everyone else to fix it, my obsessing faded fast. As I stopped being a victim with family and even co-workers by putting boundaries in place and treating me well, I felt in control of what I participated in and he didn't even figure.

Do not give up on you. Keeping tabs indicates a loss of hope that appears to be symbolised by your ex failing to meet your hopes and expectations and you taking it to a new level and deciding that there is no hope for you if you can't correct this situation. What have you lost hope about? Is it fair to have drawn this conclusion? Invest time and energy into nurturing you for a few months (put in 100% effort) and then see if you have the same loss of hope. Remember, don't be afraid to seek professional help to put things back into perspective and give you back your power.

Nurture and take care of you. When you feel the need to keep track of an entity that is outside of your control with their own motivations and life, and you're not working for the CIA, FBI or MI5, it's because in your time of need, instead of taking care of you, you're engaging in neglect. You've decided that you can only reinstate any sense of care and love if you regain control of your 'target' and acquire their attention and love, even though they're resisting it. Take. Care. Of. You. Even if you fight it immediately, you need to pour every ounce of care and concern into you and redirect the energy that you're spending elsewhere. Listen with love to yourself instead of criticism, cry and then hug yourself, comfort and console you with kind words instead trying to come up with a revenge plan and punishing yourself. Eat well, reintegrate with your friends and family, tell them how you're feeling (the trusted ones), take up a sport or go for walks or jog – exercise is a great de-stresser.

Accept that personal boundaries are being violated, something you yourself would not like to experience. Boundaries are a fundamental component of a respectful relationship.

Practice gratitude. If you feel like you have nothing to lose and nothing to be thankful for, you need to find one thing a day for the next thirty days that you are thankful for, and make sure that you write something different each day. What do you value? What do you appreciate? What are you thankful that you've been spared from today or in the future? What do you have? You have something and may even have a lot of things – what are they? Look at your life with fresh eyes and look away from your ex at least once a day to remind yourself of what you're here for – you have a greater purpose than controlling an ex. Learn to value you and the one life you have to live.

Don't make a permanent judgement about yourself. Judge the situation and see the lessons in it, but do not write yourself off because you've experienced the breakup or have been keeping track. You're human, you love, you want to be loved, and sometimes, like all humans, you don't cope that well. This is one of those times. Love you, don't hurt you. Forgive you.

Find the humour in it. Sometimes taking a good hard look at the situation can have you laughing your head off. I remember wanting to know what my ex with the girlfriend was doing, who he was talking to, which girl he was spending 'too much' time with etc. One day, it suddenly dawned on me – if his own girlfriend has no idea what the hell he's doing, how the hell could I hope to be in control of someone who I'd certainly been unable to control or know every move when we were 'together'? It suddenly seemed so ridiculous and I wept laughing. I had to laugh even harder when I contemplated telling him that I was planning to move back to Ireland or that I was really ill – when you know things have got that bad that you'd need to start doing things that you'd cringe if someone else was doing it, you know it's time to flush and make a fast exit. It's not because it's another indictment of how unworthy you are; it's a reflection of how unhealthy the relationship was.

As soon as your mind begins wandering to the obsessive zone, it's time to pull yourself up and pause for a few moments to gather yourself. Don't just run with it.

You don't want anyone's love via guilting them and this is exactly what you'll be doing if you become angry and attempt to coerce him and control his agenda. You don't want a boyfriend, lover, friend or anything where you've harassed them into their role.

What's the worst that can happen? Is it happening right now? Looking at what you have to be grateful in your life (get cracking on your daily notes of gratitude), how much does it really matter, because I can tell you, your ex, much as you cared, he is just one person. He's just not *that* special and how much of an impact he has on your life and what opinion you have of you, is wholly and solely down to you. It does not have to be like this – it doesn't.

SOME FINAL THOUGHTS FOR

KICKING THE DREAMER HABIT

You and only you alone are responsible for your feelings. When you take this on board, it will bring you back to 'base' because you can't use him or anyone else as a justification for your actions. The more you 'dream', the less of a link there is between him/your relationship and what you're feeling and the more it's based on your own internal dialogue.

Upgrade your diet from crumbs to a loaf. Dreamers can operate on a very poor diet because they use their imaginings as 'water' to bloat themselves. By recognising what true intimacy, commitment and, in essence, real mutual relationships are about, it's difficult to be sustained on a crumb and water diet.

Observe them in context with others. Often when you have been 'dreaming', it turns out that while you were in your bubble, you missed out on the fact that they treat everyone else or several others in the same way.

You know when you hear lame excuses and non-answers? That's him letting you down 'gently' and hoping you take the hint. Avoid making excuses for his excuses and you will see him for what he is.

The sky hasn't fallen down yet, so while you have sold yourself short

with your Dreamer habits, you actually have to some extent survived the pain and rejections that you thought you'd never live through. Imagine (but not for too long) how much richer and full colour your life would be if you'd stick to reality, and then go and live it.

This is one of those times when empathy comes in very handy... but not in the way you think. Instead of over-empathising and making up excuses and a fairy tale, step into his shoes, consider his position and look at things from his perspective. If you don't like how your actions and his excuses look through his eyes, this is your wake-up call. If they don't look like love and look more akin to desperation, it's because you've strayed too far. Come home!

Of course it feels like you're not going to recover from the rejection – it's because you're not recovering from the rejection. Instead, you're withdrawing into your own world, giving yourself a hard time and remaining numb. The more you feel out all the feelings that arise from rejection, is the more you gain the confidence that you can and will survive and don't take it so much to heart.

Think of all the times when you have said NO, turned someone down, broken it off, and not reciprocated the attraction. Write down each incident. You had a legitimate reason for your actions – what were they? Now even though the other person may not have understood, that doesn't change the legitimacy of your right to have said NO for whatever the reason. You didn't need a perfect reason, you just needed a reason. People, including you, do not always make rational decisions about why they aren't interested – just like you'd expect someone to respect your wishes if the shoes were on your feet, you must respect their wishes.

Don't think of yourself as weak, helpless or powerless – you're strong. You're in possession of emotional backbone – you're just not using it and even if you think it's gone, you can grow one with some boundaries and self-love. You're not frailer than everyone else or 'not as good' – stand tall in reality.

The best way to start to learn to overcome your avoidance of rejection is to use your energies to genuinely learn to take care of yourself so that you can like and love you. Spend time around consistent, solid friends and family, and start working towards a middle ground, as opposed to an extreme that has you seeing rejection in even the most innocuous of comments and actions. Setting boundaries, recognising inappropriate and unhealthy behaviour and not making yourself the centre of other people's actions goes a hell of a long way to disabling the derailing effect that living a life of Rejection Avoidance can cause.

Always remember that you're not looking to create a whole new you from scratch – you are already more than enough and the work you do going forward will allow you to reclaim the great you that's already within. That's not a dream; that's a reality.

Don't forget to visit Baggage Reclaim (baggagereclaim.com) for a wealth of posts on a variety of subjects that will help you to live and love with your self-esteem in tow.

Also check out the following:

facebook.com/baggagereclaim
youtube.com/baggagereclaim
twitter.com/nataliemlue or twitter.com/baggagereclaim

84150510R00146

Made in the USA
San Bernardino, CA
04 August 2018